TO HEIGHTS AND UNTO DEPTHS

FATHER JOHN NEPIL

To Heights and unto Depths

Letters from the Colorado Trail

IGNATIUS PRESS   SAN FRANCISCO

Cover photograph by Casey Van Pelt

Cover design by Enrique J. Aguilar

© 2025 by Ignatius Press, San Francisco
All rights reserved
ISBN 978-1-62164-741-6 (PB)
ISBN 978-1-64229-325-8 (eBook)
Library of Congress Control Number 2024950203
Printed in the United States of America ∞

To my dad

See that you make everything according
to the pattern which was shown
you on the mountain.

Hebrews 8:5

CONTENTS

FOREWORD

by Archbishop Emeritus Charles Chaput

Writing about his conversion, the author Paul Kingsnorth spoke of his need to escape, if only for a few hours or days, from a world that "denies God and launches salvo after salvo daily against the human soul". He longed for "a wild Christianity", a faith alive with the fertility and beauty of nature in a deadening age of the Machine. "I feel like I am being firmly pointed", he said, "day after day, back toward ... the song that is sung quietly through the land by its maker, the song that is in the stream running, in the mist wreathing the crags, the growling of the rooks, the thunder over the mountains."[1]

J. R. R. Tolkien and C. S. Lewis had the same thoughts. Both lived through the mechanized devastation of Europe in the First World War. Both came away from it intensely aware of the divine hand in Creation. As a result, both authors filled their fiction with the beauty of a vivid natural world: walking forests, teeming rivers, nymphs, talking animals, and above all, mountains that are majestic, forbidding, and "holy"—holy in the original Hebrew meaning of the word. Mountains are *other than* everyday human life. They point to Someone higher, and things that are greater, than themselves.

[1] Paul Kingsnorth, "A Wild Christianity", *First Things*, March 2023, https://www.firstthings.com/article/2023/03/a-wild-christianity.

In Lewis' *Chronicles of Narnia*, the lion Aslan (the figure of Jesus) is a good lion, but not a tame one. Likewise the Colorado Rockies are "good" mountains, in the sense of their beauty and their healing balm for the spirit. But they are not tame. And no one understands that better, or writes about it with more style and Christian faith, than the man who wrote the book in your hands.

I've known John Nepil—now Father John Nepil—since his high school years. I ordained and posted him to his first parish in Boulder, Colorado. It was there that his creative priestly ministry in Colorado's backcountry took shape. John describes his book as a reflection on mountaineering and theology. What that translates to, for the reader, is an immersion in the "Book of Nature", along with the books of Scripture, to encounter the living God.

The setting is the Colorado Trail: roughly 500 miles of demanding terrain, ascending and descending across eight mountain ranges and multiple valleys, nearly all above 9,000 feet. Father John made the trek with several friends. He was joined for various segments of the journey by other priests and young laymen. The result is a unique kind of "fraternity of the trail"—a pilgrimage of the high places—and a guidebook to the spiritual heart of nature's grandeur. In effect, the reader joins that fraternity, that *pilgrimage*, and deepens a Catholic understanding of the world and the Author of its beauty along the way. It's a marvelous read.

Having said that, I do have a confession. When asked to write this foreword, I hesitated. I admire Father John a great deal, but worried that I wouldn't like the material. I grew up in America's flatland—Kansas—and I've never felt comfortable in the mountains. I know very little about camping and hiking, and I've never experienced a "Rocky Mountain high" except in song. I thought this book might be foreign to me. Exactly the opposite is the case. And the reason is simple: I read these pages with Psalm 8 in the back of my head. In praising God, the Psalmist says:

> When I look at your heavens, the work of your fingers
> the moon and the stars which you have established;
> what is man that you are mindful of him,
> and the son of man that you care for him?
> Yet you have made him little less than the angels,
> and you have crowned him with glory and honor. (vv. 3–5)

Creation is an expression of God's love, and the natural world is a gift to man to be shepherded by humanity's stewardship—which in turn reminds man of his meaning and dignity. The central questions of our age all boil down to what it means to be human. Do our lives have any purpose beyond consuming what we can, as soon as we can? How can we remain human when we're swarmed with new technologies that cocoon and disconnect us from any intimacy with the actual, physical world?

In the face of today's confusion, Father John shows us the importance of removing ourselves from the culture of noise, if only for a while, and going to the silence and beauty of nature, just as Jesus did. It's a renewal strategy for both our sanity and our spiritual lives, and he demonstrates its power in an exciting, adventurous way.

It's especially worth noting this book's title. Height and depth play a key role in our perception of the material world. Height is the measurement from the base to the top of something. It's about zeniths and summits. Depth measures the space from the surface to the deepest part of something. It's about volume and substance. These same two words have value in understanding our spiritual lives. God calls us to the heights of a "new creation" (2 Cor 5:17). But we get there only if we move from the surface to the deepest parts of our human reality. God calls us to go forward (higher) and inward (deeper) toward the joy of his kingdom. A spiritual life without that effort can never be more than flat and shallow.

My own life as a Christian, priest, and bishop owes a great debt to Pope Saint John Paul II. Throughout his ministry, John Paul loved the mountains, beginning with the Tatra Mountains of his homeland, Poland. He found joy in hiking and camping there with the young people he loved and served. It was there that he began to develop his grasp of the "new evangelization" by which he led so many others to encounter God and experience a spiritual rebirth. Father John's book leads us in the same direction; it's a gift that helps us imagine and desire a similar path for ourselves. His story of hiking with friends in the glory of God's creation and of embracing difficult goals together— the heights and the depths—leads us to the foundational Christian mystery of the Incarnation where God, Creation, and mankind come to be known together. It's what makes the book remarkable. And it's why you need to read it.

+ Charles J. Chaput, O.F.M. Cap.
Archbishop Emeritus of Philadelphia
Solemnity of Christ the King, 2024

PROLOGUE

It was an unusually cold night for late August. My dad and I had arrived at the foot of Mount Elbert and just finished setting up our tent. Climbing inside, I reached into my light blue Kelty external frame Pack, which felt oddly spacious, as if something were missing. With increasing panic, I began pulling everything out until, at last, I realized it—I had forgotten my sleeping bag.

I immediately concluded that the most reasonable option and only chance of survival was to coerce my dad into giving me his. With the most sincere and pathetic look I could muster, I turned to my dad and said, "Uh, Dad, I forgot my sleeping bag."

My father, a West Point graduate and career military officer, turned to me and with the utmost paternal sobriety said, "Son, tonight you are going to learn a life lesson."

A life lesson learned. That night was the worst night of sleep in my life, and I vowed never to forget my sleeping bag again.

We rose before dawn to begin a steady climb up Mount Elbert, the highest peak in Colorado and penultimate highest in the contiguous United States. I was unfortunately too sleep-deprived to notice how majestic that morning was; hovering clouds hid the valley below, giving the numinous impression that one was truly in Heaven.

We summited, descended, and returned to Denver. I made a second vow that day: never to climb a mountain again; and, if possible, never to return to the mountains at all.

That was twenty-five years ago. Though keeping my first vow never to forget my sleeping bag, I have been unfaithful to the second. As the fatigue and pain of that climb up Mount Elbert wore off, something was born in me, something sparked. I realized then that I was utterly captivated by the irresistible and inexpressible desire for the heights. Something was awakened—a fire that could not be subdued.

I set out with the full vigor of youth to conquer the high peaks of Colorado. The Colorado Rockies are the rooftop of the American West; for here you find fifty-four peaks that rise above 14,000 feet (hence the name fourteeners). To summit all of them was a feat that only a thousand men and women had accomplished, and I was determined to join their ranks.[1]

At that time, my Catholic upbringing had no bearing on my adventures in the backcountry. In fact, it was something I was desperately trying to rid myself of. In the beginning, I climbed mountains unreflectively, simply because they provided an enjoyment unlike any other. But as I grew older, I realized I was attempting something spiritual in the mountains, a refuge from the cutthroat academic, athletic, and social pressures of my suburban milieu. I was searching for a way to *transcend* my problems and sought to do so on mountain ascents. From the Latin words *scandere* (to climb) and *trans* (across, beyond), I thought I could

---

[1] The numbering of Colorado's fourteeners is debated anywhere between fifty-two and seventy-four. When I first began climbing fourteeners, a peak was designated by a 300-foot topographical prominence (meaning that the saddle between mountains must drop at least 300 feet). Accordingly, there were officially fifty-two listed fourteeners. But given the utter distinctiveness of North Maroon Peak and El Diente, the climbing community added them, settling the count at fifty-four. Lately, it has become fashionable to count fifty-eight (and thereby removing the rule of prominence). But the Colorado Mountain Club still holds to the list of fifty-four, as do I. They also keep the official count of those who have completed the fourteeners. When I finished in 2013, I was listed as number 1156.

transcend the small and petty things of life by "climbing beyond them".

But there was a problem: the more I climbed, the more frustrated and disenchanted I became. At the heights I was glimpsing something real, but only for a moment, and then I returned home even more unsatisfied. Later, the author G. K. Chesterton would put words to my experience: "Take away the supernatural, and what remains is the unnatural."[2] My spiritual attempt, infused with a spirit of conquest and self-validation, made me feel all the more unnatural in my humanity. The supernatural was missing, and, deep down, I knew I needed a remedy.

By a series of truly unbelievable circumstances, I came to a moment of decision and faced my Catholic upbringing squarely in the face. What I found remains to this day the most astonishing and surprising reality I have ever experienced—Jesus Christ is the true revelation of God and one that can be known in its fullness through the Catholic Church. The event of Christ, a newfound encounter in my life, now set the trajectory for all things and became the sole key to the interpretation of my every love, the answer to my every question.

In the years that followed, I discerned a call to the priesthood and entered a seminary. There I met Father Raymond Gawronski, an eclectic and brilliant Jesuit, himself a lover of the outdoors. My spiritual director for the next decade, he formed in me a Catholic vision of reality, teaching me that "the book of nature" (together with "the book of Scripture") was a place I could read to discover the living God.[3] In the spring of 2016, Father Gawronski was diagnosed with stage 4 cancer and died forty days later.

---

[2] G. K. Chesterton, "Heretics", in *The Collected Works of G. K. Chesterton*, vol. 1 (San Francisco: Ignatius Press, 1986), 88.

[3] Cf. Pope John Paul II, Encyclical Letter *Fides et Ratio* (September 14, 1998), no. 19.

I will likely never recover from his absence in my life. But his life and teaching, his laughter and fatherly love, still echo in my heart on every mountain climb.

When I became a priest, I thought I would have to renounce my love of the backcountry. But precisely the opposite occurred; the passionate fire for the heights only quickened. I had climbed all the fourteeners; now my greatest joy and noblest ambition was to celebrate Mass on their every summit.

In the twenty years since I converted back to the faith, I have desired to write on the experience of God in backcountry adventure. But the actual writing of the book has proved more daunting than any climb. There are books on mountaineering and books on Catholic theology; but never, it appears, the twain shall meet. Moreover, writing now as a theologian, there are popular works and academic works—and much to the frustration of friends and editors, this can be categorized as neither. The task before me is what we call in climbing a "first ascent", a new and unclimbed route up a mountain. As the attempt is being done by a novice writer (even less skilled in the interior life), one hopes that it will at least cut a trail for those more capable to follow. I am, nonetheless, indebted to the many thinkers whose names will appear throughout these pages—Luigi Giussani, Joseph Ratzinger, Dietrich von Hildebrand, and Hans Urs von Balthasar, to name a few. It was their thought that I found synthesized in the life of Father Gawronski and now attempt to make my own. They remain the true masters and guides on the theological trail that leads to God.

Most importantly, I am obliged to two books from which I drew profound inspiration as a young man: Romano Guardini's *Letters from Lake Como* and Hilaire Belloc's *The Path to Rome*. Our attempt is a tall one: to take the epistolary style of a Guardini and infuse it with the venturous narrative of a Belloc. They provided me with the central project of this book—"the attempt to view the pattern of Christian existence as a whole".[4]

If this typographic "first ascent" is to unite alpine adventure and Catholic theology, it does so with a particular question in mind. Why are a great number of young people, raised either Catholic or in other Christian denominations, abandoning the faith wholesale by the time they reach early adulthood? A recent study found that 34 percent of Americans, raised Catholic, no longer identify with the faith of their childhood.[5] Many times, these former Catholics are calling themselves "nones"—persons who, when asked their religious affiliation, check "none". This fast-growing sociological phenomenon is a symptom of a monumental cultural shift happening in our day. But it has been happening for centuries, as John Henry Newman described in the mid-1800s:

> A great number of men live and die without reflecting at all upon the state of things in which they find themselves. They take things as they come, and follow their inclinations as far as they have the opportunity. They are guided mainly by pleasure and pain, not by reason, principle, or conscience; and they do not attempt to *interpret* this world, to determine what it means, or to reduce what they see and feel to system.[6]

We moderns seem to have grown tired of interpreting the world, especially through the religious tradition of

---

[4] R. Guardini, *Freedom, Grace, and Destiny: Three Chapters in the Interpretation of Existence*, trans. John Murray, S.J. (New York: Pantheon Books, 1961), 9.

[5] S. Bullivant, *Mass Exodus: Catholic Disaffiliation in Britain and America since Vatican II* (Oxford: Oxford University Press, 2019), 2.

[6] J. H. Newman, "The Cross of Christ, the Measure of the World", in *Parochial and Plain Sermons* (San Francisco: Ignatius Press, 1997), 1239.

Christianity. And in the Church, we reinforce this fatigue by reducing the faith to merely "doing Catholic things". In our estimation, this is a systemic cause of the rising phenomenon of the "none".

Our world is now post-Christian, no longer permeated by an operative vision of reality informed by Christian faith. For this reason, it is insufficient simply to raise "practicing Catholics"—we have to instill a Catholic worldview. We can no longer afford to propose Christianity as a duty; it must be, above all, an attraction. Without this transformation in Catholic formation, future generations will become "nones", the statistics of secularization. We must begin again by cultivating a Catholic worldview in the hearts and minds of young people. And one of the best places to do this is in the backcountry.

What, then, is a worldview? Joseph Ratzinger explains it as "a synthesis of knowledge and values, which together propose to us a total vision of the real".[7] Knowledge that informs the intellect and values that move the will, when synthesized, offer a coherent vision of reality. This means that intellectual and moral conversion to the Gospel is central to a Catholic worldview. It is something that, like a mountain climb, requires serious effort and the surest of guides.

Now the very notion of a worldview is difficult to grasp because it is so foundational. In fact, there is nothing more basic, or more influential in our life, than our worldview. From this hidden fusion of knowledge and values comes my every decision—from the person I marry, to the hobbies I enjoy, even to what I eat for breakfast. More powerfully, it determines how I love and the path I choose toward the fulfillment of my desires.

---

[7] J. Ratzinger, *Daughter Zion: Meditations on the Church's Marian Belief*, trans. John M. McDermott, S.J. (San Francisco: Ignatius Press, 1983), 57.

A worldview is the source from which I interpret my life as meaningful. Ultimately, a worldview addresses the presuppositional questions that arise from my inner religious sense. These questions—where I am from, where I am going, and is anything meaningful in between— necessarily involve the question of God and will determine my relationship to him.

Long before the time of Christ, the ancient Greeks had a revolutionary "break-through" on the level of worldview. They discovered something called *being* and set their entire vision of reality upon it. Known as metaphysics, the study of being became the grounds upon which one came to know and interpret the things of the world. And in the earliest days of Christianity, the Church aligned, not with the cult of pagan gods, but with the God of the philosophers—those who pursued truth, goodness, and beauty as paths toward the totality of the real. With the revelation of Christ as the Word [*logos*] (Jn 1:1), metaphysics was supernaturally elevated to become theology— faith seeking to understand the mystery of all things in God. The Christian worldview is, then, by necessity, both metaphysical and theological. As my Italian professor once said, "When you go to the restaurant and choose between steak or fish, you are doing metaphysics." And when we climb high up in the alpine regions of the world, we are doing theology. As Luigi Giussani describes, this offers a new experience of reality: "Since I am part of the reality of Christ, I look at the mountains, the morning and the evening, all reality, looking first for the ultimate root in everything I see. And the conviction that the truth is in me and with me makes me extremely positive about everything."[8]

---

[8] L. Giussani, S. Alberto, and J. Prades, *Generating Traces in the History of the World: New Traces in the Christian Experience*, trans. Patrick Stevenson (Montreal: McGill-Queen's University Press, 2010), 116.

In addition, human beings are relational, meaning we form worldviews in and through community. Following the most important formation in family life, it is in the community of friends that young people learn to synthesize knowledge and values. For me personally, the years of backcountry adventures, so crucial to my Catholic worldview, were unimaginable without a community of faith. Together we set out for high peaks and returned with, in the words of Guardini, "a living pattern of a spiritual reality".[9] They were experiences of new discovery and re-enchantment, absolutely thrilling and utterly compelling. Though the patterns of the Catholic worldview are many, there lie within it three great discoveries.

First, the discovery of humanity: Anyone who goes into the backcountry knows of its restorative power. No technological screen can provide the feeling of a cool summer breeze melodically passing through an aspen grove. No digital photograph can capture the majesty of high peaks in morning alpenglow. We must leave the cities of concrete and glass to recover again our most basic and instinctive desire to be human. But as I mentioned above, simply the experience of creation is not enough to satisfy the human heart—we are made for relationship with creation's very source. Into this human need poured God's ultimate gift, Jesus Christ, God made man. He remains "the way, and the truth, and the life" (Jn 14:6) of all that is authentically human. This, then, is our first task: "Before all else," says Guardini, "man's depths must be awakened."[10]

Second, the discovery of creation: With a Christian understanding of humanity, we gain a new awareness of

[9] R. Guardini, *The Living God*, trans. Stanley Godman (New York: Pantheon, 1957), 13.
[10] R. Guardini, *The End of the Modern World*, trans. Joseph Theman and Herbert Burke (Wilmington: ISI Books, 1998), 215.

how created things present themselves. We find them alive and speaking. The poet Gerard Manley Hopkins called this *inscape*—that concrete things disclose themselves in a totally unique form, revealing an unfathomably intelligent design. The word they speak is that they were created, and thus they speak of a Creator. Unlike other worldviews that attempt to move beyond creation, the Judeo-Christian tradition affirms that the uncreated Creator is known in and through creation. Only the experience of creation in the Creator corresponds to the desire of the human heart. Or, in the words of Joseph Ratzinger, "creatureliness is the measure of man."[11]

Third, the discovery of God: When Nietzsche proclaimed his famous war cry "God is dead", he spoke of something true. In our modern world, we have reduced God to an idea, to an abstraction—and, in fact, killed him. Marked by a process of secularization (eclipsing the supernatural), we have all lost the God-question and must actively recover it for ourselves. Thus, we must go into creation to rediscover our humanity and, in doing so, encounter God in Jesus Christ. In him we see the nuptial unity of humanity and divinity, the wedding place of true communion and Trinitarian love. What we find in revelation is this: when man's desire for God is ascending to the heights, it is encountered in God's descending love, as he heads for the depths. At this meeting point lies the fulfillment of our humanity. As Guardini concludes, bringing us full circle: "Only he who knows God will understand man."[12]

[11] J. Ratzinger, *The Divine Project: Reflections on Creation and the Church*, trans. Chase Faucheux (San Francisco: Ignatius Press, 2023), 100.

[12] R. Guardini as quoted in H. U. von Balthasar, *Romano Guardini: Reform from the Source*, trans. Albert K. Wimmer and D. C. Schindler (San Francisco: Ignatius Press, 2010), 42.

But there is one final conclusion to be drawn. Humanity, creation, and God come together in a single mystery—the Incarnation. This is the central key of the Christian worldview, that moment when God becomes man and enters into creation: "And the Word became flesh and dwelt among us" (Jn 1:14). This book has one purpose: to re-propose to modern man that the Incarnate Word is the interpretative key to reality. All three—humanity, creation, and God—stand or fall with our acceptance or rejection of this most seminal truth.

The setting of our story is the Colorado Trail. Described as "the trail to nowhere", the Colorado Trail was a series of disconnected paths that, coming together in 1987, traverses horizontally across the Colorado Rockies. Spanning 486 miles, it crosses eight mountain ranges, ascending nearly 90,000 feet in elevation and descending the same. It begins in a passageway just southwest of Denver and concludes on the other side of the Rockies in the town of Durango. Holding to the Continental Divide and remaining mostly above 9,000 feet, it is considered by many to be the most beautiful of America's long-distance trails.

In July of 2022, I resolved with three men to undertake the challenge of the Colorado Trail in the form of a "thru-hike" (i.e., doing it in one go). Other groups of priests and young men would join us along the way and make up part of the adventure to be recollected in these letters. Additionally, as the Colorado Trail passed through certain ranges and valleys, I could not help but recall many of the stories for my fourteener climbs. Some are noble, others ridiculous—but all of them provided those earliest perceptions of the truly unthinkable: that the Catholic worldview offers the fullest spiritual vision of the backcountry;

and the backcountry, a most privileged place for Catholic education.

These letters tell the story of our journey on the Colorado Trail. But this story of the trail is likewise a theological guidebook, written for those seeking a deeper spiritual vision of the mountains. It is written for all who love the backcountry and desire to recover the great patrimony of humanity, largely lost to modernity. Above all, these letters propose the vision of the Catholic worldview and invite you to embrace it as a way of life.

Let us then set out on the Colorado Trail, that in encountering the love of Christ, we may be led to heights and unto depths (cf. Eph 3:18–19).

TO HEIGHTS

It was the summer solstice, that day when the Earth's orbit tilts fully toward the sun and the world is filled with light. I stepped onto the trail with my companions in a burst of enthusiasm; but quickly it was subsumed into a reverential solemnity. It felt as if we were going into battle. But as those first miles passed, all trepidations were calmed by lush serenity and cool morning air. Dew held fiercely to the leaves of the rolling hillside, as the rush of Indian Creek spoke the words of Hopkins: "There lives the dearest fresh-ness, deep down things."[1] The moment was nothing short of Edenic, the first gift and consolation of the trail. Our hearts lifted as we began to climb.

Our first day on the Colorado Trail was a gradual entry into the foothills of the Rockies, a thirteen-mile march that would cover the first few thousand feet of elevation.[2] As we turned westward and climbed out of the valley floor, we ascended a series of rolling hills and soon reposed at a

[1] G. M. Hopkins, "God's Grandeur", in *As Kingfishers Catch Fire* (New York: Penguin Books, 1918), 1.

[2] For much of 2022, Waterton Canyon, the traditional starting point of the Colorado Trail, was closed for maintenance by Denver Water. Hikers were thus re-routed to the other side of Roxborough State Park to begin at Indian Creek Trailhead. Though initially disappointed, we were grateful to replace the flat dirt of the first 6.7 miles in Waterton Canyon with the more varied terrain found east of Lenny's Rest.

place called Lenny's Rest. From there, we looked eastward through the narrow valley of the South Platte and took in the last view of the city and our home.

In the next six days, we would steadily ascend over the contours of the Front Range before arriving at Georgia Pass, our first touch of treeline and the meeting place of the Continental Divide. This trajectory raised the initial question of the trail: What led us here, this ineffable draw to the heights?

As long as man has walked the earth, he has felt this innate sense of wonder and awe in the mountains. They spoke of something divine, awakening his consciousness for something beyond this world. Unlike every other creature, man finds himself restless in creation; he desires to encounter it as mystery, to interpret it as meaningful, and to discover within himself the call to transcendence.

This is our first word on mountains—like all great works of art, they have meaning but not purpose.[3] In a world dominated by industry and technology, where everything is reduced to the purposes of man, we retreat to the heights precisely because they are purposeless. City life, filled as it is with concrete and glass, speak of artificial constructs—not the meaningfulness of the real. Mountains simply *are*, and by naturally being, they mean something.

"We must begin from above," writes von Balthasar, "from the heights, in order then to see how the divine beauty gradually penetrates and elevates all depths of reality."[4] From the ever-expansive view of a mountain summit,

---

[3] Cf. H. U. von Balthasar, "The Marian Principle", in *Communio* 15 (Spring 1988): 128.

[4] H. U. von Balthasar, *The Glory of the Lord: A Theological Aesthetics*, vol. 1, *Seeing the Form*, trans. Erasmo Leiva-Merikakis (San Francisco: Ignatius Press, 1982), 106.

man is drawn out from the smallness of things back into the full breadth of the created realm. In this way he is categorically different from all other living things. This call to the heights, intrinsic to the heart of man, makes him decidedly and undeniably *religious*, a word that has fallen out of favor in our modern day. Man is inescapably compelled by his innate religiosity. In this way, religion is not an elective affinity, but, as Luigi Giussani describes, a *sense*. Just as we engage reality through physical senses, so too do we interpret meaningfulness through a religious sense. Man has a different kind of soul, one that is rational and created immediately by God. This configures him as a religious being, which Giussani defines as his "ultimate desire, the desire to know the origin and meaning of existence".[5] Religion alone elevates the experience of human life; and it is in this context that the Christian claim must be re-presented. The heart of man is made to search for the heights.

The Garden of Eden was on a mountaintop (Gen 2:8–15).[6] Four rivers flow out from it; and rivers, by nature, descend. If, then, humanity was born at the heights, it makes sense that we are always trying to get back to them. In the ancient world, mythological sagas and epic poetry expressed this natural religiosity, ascribing sacredness to the heights. This is likewise the case with the revelation of the God of Israel in the Old Covenant. First, we see Abraham ascending Mount Moriah to offer the sacrifice of his son (Gen 22). Then Moses, who first encounters the living God on "the mountain of God" (Ex 3), later returns

---

[5] L. Giussani, *At the Origin of the Christian Claim*, trans. Viviane Hewitt (Montreal: McGill-Queen's University Press, 1998), 4.

[6] Cf. J. Bergsma and B. Pitre, *A Catholic Introduction to the Bible*, vol. 1, *The Old Testament* (San Francisco: Ignatius Press, 2018), 102: "Eden is described as a mountain or mountaintop—this can be deduced from the fact that all four primary rivers of the earth (from the Israelite perspective) flow out *from* Eden." This is likewise the vision of Dante, who places the Earthly Paradise at the top of the Mount of Purgatory (cf. Dante, *Purgatorio*, Canto 27).

to receive the Law and found a new covenant (Ex 19). Having established themselves, the Israelites build the holy city of Jerusalem on Mount Zion. At last, the prophets point us to the heights, for when the Messiah comes as a shepherd, he will pasture them on mountain heights (Ezek 34). In the Psalms, Israel fulfills man's innate religiosity in its covenantal prayer: "I lift up my eyes to the hills. From where does my help come? My help comes from the Lord, who made heaven and earth" (Ps 121:1–2).

When God became man "when the time had fully come" (Gal 4:4), mountains continued as the privileged backdrop for his saving work. At the onset of his public ministry, Jesus is taken up a high mountain to be tempted by Satan (Mt 4). He regularly sought the mountaintop as a place of prayer and fellowship with his apostles (Mk 3). On the Mount of the Beatitudes, Christ teaches and bestows upon them the New Law in the Sermon on the Mount (Mt 5). On Mount Tabor, Christ's divinity radiates as he is transfigured before them (Mt 17). And lastly, Jesus dies as an atoning sacrifice upon the Mount of Calvary (Lk 23).

Mountains are now drawn to the apex of their religious imagery, being the place where Christ calls us to "be with him" and to remain as his companions (Mk 3:13–14). This is a foretaste of Heaven; for as Scripture begins on a mountaintop, so too does it conclude: "And in the Spirit he carried me away to a great, high mountain, and showed me the holy city Jerusalem coming down out of heaven from God" (Rev 21:10).

The idea to thru-hike the Colorado Trail started a year ago, over beers with a guy named Cody. It is to him that I owe the idea, and without him I never would have accomplished it. We spent a year poring over maps and obsessing over gear, talking through the plan over the countless hours of mundane training hikes. It was from our friendship that this trip was born.

Cody is, nonetheless, a rather difficult figure to describe. After a relatively normal suburban upbringing, he went to college in Montana, joined the Army, and was sent to Alaska to serve in an Arctic Warfare Unit. It was here that he became a skilled outdoorsman of the first rank—fly fishing for salmon, hunting caribou, and occasionally running from grizzly bears. His capacity to endure suffering, pain, and cold was unlike anything I had ever seen. After his military tour, he set out to live the dream—travel and adventure, a life free of responsibility and dependence. He hiked the Camino de Santiago and the Pacific Crest Trail (from Mexico to Canada) before setting sail to circumnavigate the globe.

This is when I met him. Every six months or so, he would return home, and, over drinks, we would discuss the deeper questions of life. Shortly after college, Cody had converted to Catholicism—so despite being a hardlining G.I., he had a deep affectivity and a real heart. Beneath a stoic countenance, there was a man searching for God. Like me, he had lived for the pursuit of adventure and was ever restless. What he desired was what Kierkegaard called a "deeper immersion in existence".[7] And the Colorado Trail was the prime opportunity for this transformation.

Cody walked behind me that first afternoon, and I could feel he was nervous. With each section of the trail, I had invited a random collection of priests, friends, and young

[7] As quoted in H. de Lubac, *The Drama of Atheist Humanism*, trans. Edith M. Riley, Anne Englund Nash, and Mark Sebanc (San Francisco: Ignatius Press, 1995), 111.

men to join us. Our initial group of nine (nicknamed "the Fellowship" due to their uncanny resemblance to *Lord of the Rings* characters) would accompany the thru-hikers for the first five days, until we reached our first resupply at Kenosha Pass. We knew that every group was a major risk—but watching this first one stagger through the heat of the first afternoon gave us both cause for concern. We had spent the year in training and preparation for a thru-hike; but there was no guarantee each group had done the same.

Having passed through an endless array of forested switchbacks, we now rested at a series of cliff bands, which, facing west, gave us the first opportunity to breathe in a mountain vista. By evening, the Fellowship arrived at the South Platte River, and we made our first camp. We rejoiced at the encounter with "trail magic", a tradition where past thru-hikers appear on the trail, offering Coca-Cola, Snickers bars, and the like. The first day was over, and the river crossed. It felt like a milestone; for just as the hobbits crossed the Brandywine, leaving the safety and comforts of Hobbiton, we had left home and headed deeper into the unknown of the Colorado wilderness.

2

THE MOUNTAINS ARE CALLING

In May of 1996, the human-induced Buffalo Creek wildfire burned nearly 12,000 acres of Pike National Forest. Two months later, a massive thunderstorm swept through the region resulting in severe flooding and the final destruction of an already ravaged landscape. At the center of this tragedy ran the Colorado Trail, on which we were to pass on the second day.

Knowing this to be our hottest and driest day on the trail, we rose at 3:30 a.m. and climbed up to an elevated plain high above the river valley floor. Undulating our way between Raleigh Peak and the Chair Rocks, the terrain was utterly lunar—arid and desolate, giving no appearance of life. This spectral, incinerated landscape would last eleven miles, a passage largely consumed by desperate thoughts and a desire to find water. We drew confidence from the poetic intuition of von Balthasar: "The world has become a heap of fragments. But every single splinter remains precious, and from each fragment there flashes a ray of the mystery of its origin."[1] Even in this barren wasteland, the inexhaustible beauty of nature's origins still spoke with resilience and tenacity.

---

[1] H. U. von Balthasar, *Heart of the World*, trans. Erasmo S. Leiva (San Francisco: Ignatius Press, 1979), 20.

"The mountains are calling, and I must go." These words from the environmental philosopher and political conservationist John Muir are as iconic in outdoor culture as they are cliché. Though the words resonate and inspire many, few have interpreted their deeper meaning. Addressed to his sister from Yosemite in September 1873, the full text of Muir's letter reads as follows:

> The Scotch are slow, but some day I will have the results of my mountain studies in a form in which you all will be able to read & judge of them. In the mean time, I write occasionally for the Overland Monthly, but neither these magazine articles nor my first book will form any finished part of the scientific contribution that I hope to make.... The mountains are calling & I must go, & I will work on while I can, studying incessantly.[2]

John Muir was a remarkable and noble figure. Born in Scotland, he immigrated to Wisconsin in 1849 before heading west at the age of thirty to become a sheepherder in the valley of Yosemite. He was no restless wanderer, but a true autodidact, up at four in the morning reading before the day's work began. The call of the mountains, which he felt so strongly, was not a call to casual enjoyment and the pursuit of adventure; it was a call to personal renunciation and the service of creation. His incessant study as a naturalist was the response to the call, advocating constantly for its preservation. It was for this reason that shortly after writing this letter to his sister, he left his beloved Yosemite to reside permanently in Oakland. All for the sake of his writing and championing the cause of the natural parks. All this because he heard a call.

[2] J. Muir, *Letter to Sarah (Muir Galloway)*, September 3, 1873.

Muir had a complex relationship with Christianity. Raised in the harsh spiritual climate of Scotch Calvinism, he went in search of a worldview that corresponded to his deep love affair with nature. Here he discovered the philosophical movement of Transcendentalism, which, at the time, had become widely influential in the American East. Its two most famous proponents, Ralph Waldo Emerson and Henry David Thoreau, were attempting to get out of the Enlightenment's drive to rationalize the universe. Emerson, originally a Unitarian minister, stepped thoroughly beyond the parameters of Christian orthodoxy by identifying God as the soul of the world, which he called the *Over-Soul*.[3]

Transcendentalism paved the way for our present-day situation: why many hear the call of the mountains but few take interest in the caller. The question must be posed: Why is it that postmodern man, with his deep affection for nature, no longer encounters the God of Jesus Christ? The contemporary *ethos* of outdoor culture has been refashioned by nineteenth-century philosophical movements such as Transcendentalism—movements that, while giving the semblance of Christianity, have decidedly departed from it.

A call implies a person. Animals signal to one another, but humans call. A call implies language, which requires rational intelligence. A call is a communication of a *logos*—a word that is meaningful. When a Christian reads Muir's description of the call, he interprets it as a personal God speaking a *logos* through creation. God is not the soul of creation, as the Transcendentalists thought, but a being that exists outside of creation. As created being participates in the being of God, a strict line of metaphysical demarcation

---

[3] Cf. R. W. Emerson, "The Over-Soul", in *Nature and Selected Essays* (New York: Penguin Books, 2003).

is drawn: God is not creation; creation is not God. Saint
Augustine posed this in the form of a question in his *Confessions*: "I asked the earth; and it answered, 'I am not He';
and whatsoever are therein made the same confession. I
asked the sea and the deeps, and the creeping things that
lived, and they replied, 'We are not thy God, seek higher
than we' ... I asked the vast bulk of the earth of my God,
and it answered me, 'I am not He, but He made me.' "[4]

Despite being metaphysically distinct, Creator and creation are in an intimate relation; the former holds the latter
in being and reveals him as such. This metaphysical distinction, known solely through Christian revelation, was
categorically rejected at the onset of modernity. Though
thinkers like Emerson and Thoreau sought to re-found
creation in the divine, they were destined to fail without
the foundations of a Christian metaphysics of creation.

Even within the canon of Scriptures, this conclusion
took centuries to clarify. It is best attested to in the Book
of Wisdom, one of the last of the Old Testament books to
be composed.

> For from the greatness and beauty of created things
> comes a corresponding perception of their Creator.
> Yet these men are little to be blamed,
> for perhaps they go astray
> while seeking God and desiring to find him.
> For as they live among his works they keep searching,
> and they trust in what they see, because the things that
>   are seen are beautiful.
> Yet again, not even they are to be excused;
> for if they had the power to know so much
> that they could investigate the world,
> how did they fail to find sooner the Lord of these things?
>   (Wis 13:5–9)

[4] Augustine, *Confessions*, X.6.

The Christian hears in the call of creation this "corresponding perception". Men like Muir and others are to be praised for their adherence and reverence toward the beauty of things; but they are likewise not to be excused. How did they fail to discover the author and source of this call? Powerful presuppositions had altered the formation of their worldviews, the same that have affected ours. Yet even today, God is still calling—just as he has for millennia. Hearing the call of God in creation is not an aspect of the Christian faith, but one that strikes at its very heart. As von Balthasar concludes: "The essence of being a Christian is to be open daily and hourly to the call of God and to let oneself be touched and guided by it."[5]

One of the greatest mountaineers of the early twentieth century was an Italian by the name of Achille Ratti. A contemporary of John Muir, he likewise reflected on the multidimensional question of the call to the mountains:

> Is it perchance a mysterious inexplicable fascination, which leads him to defy mortal perils at every step, to risk his brave but fragile life on vast and lonely expanses of ice.... It is the feeling in him of his spiritual energy, which inspires him and drives him to overcome the terrors of lifeless matter; it is the desire to measure man's individual faculties, the infinite power of intelligent free-will, with the brute forces of the elements; it is the sacred instinct which bids us explore in the service of science the inmost structure and life of the earth, the mysterious organism of all created things.[6]

Achille Ratti was later known by another name—Pope Pius XI. As a young priest in Milan, he was famous for

[5] H. U. von Balthasar, *The Christian State of Life*, trans. Sister Mary Frances McCarthy (San Francisco: Ignatius Press, 1984), 435.

[6] A. Ratti, *Climbs on Alpine Peaks*, trans. J. E. C. Eaton (Boston: Houghton Mifflin, 1929), 40–41.

first ascents on Mont Blanc, the Matterhorn, and a variety of other truly remarkable climbs. Writing later as pope, he offers one of the most compelling Catholic responses to the question of the heights:

> Of all the activities in which men seek wholesome enjoyment, none may be said to be healthier, for the strength of body and soul alike, than a mountain ascent, provided all recklessness be avoided. For while one's strength is renewed and increased through hard labor and the struggle to reach the purer and more rarified regions of the air, it also happens that the soul, by wrestling with every type of difficulty, becomes more persistent in its handling of the burdens and duties of life. And the mind, through the contemplation of the immense and beautiful view … from the summits, more easily rises toward God, the Author and Lord of nature.[7]

From the climbing memoirs of Pope Pius XI, we rediscover a perennial truth: what begins as a silent call to the mountains resolves in the most intimate and indescribable experience of the God of the heights.

Around the time Cody and I first conceived of the idea of the Colorado Trail, I met Casey. A blend of "Minnesota nice" and Rambo, he remains one of the most paradoxical characters I have ever met. A homeschooler who enlisted in the Ranger Regiment at the age of eighteen, Casey did a tour in Afghanistan that forever shaped him. Every night for three months, he boarded a Chinook helicopter and went on mission. What he experienced there only the tattooed sleeve on his left arm could tell. Upon his return, he eventually made his way to Colorado, where I met him

---

[7] Attributed to A. Ratti, ibid.

and invited him to climb Long's Peak. When we finished the fifteen-mile, 5,000-foot Keyhole route, he looked at me and said, "That's it?" I knew then that he was a perfect candidate for the thru-hike.

Having traversed the scorched earth of Buffalo Creek, we saw what may have been a mirage—a spigot outside a volunteer fire station. It may well have been the fountain of youth, for at that moment it felt like our salvation. Shortly thereafter, we settled into camp, our reward for the day's work. Situated in a small pine grove, we looked west and, for the first time, glimpsed the high peaks. In that moment I knew what Belloc felt when he first laid eyes on the Alps:

> Let me put it thus: that from the height of Weissenstein I saw, as it were, my religion. I mean, humility, the fear of death, the terror of height and of distance, the glory of God, the infinite potentiality of reception whence springs that divine thirst of the soul; my aspiration also towards completion, and my confidence in the dual destiny.... This it is also which leads some men to climb mountaintops, but not me, for I am afraid of slipping down.[8]

To the north stood Mounts Evans and Bierstadt, majestic guardians of Colorado's sacred high country. To the south, we viewed the Tarryall Mountains, a forested bastion of the Lost Creek Wilderness and our pathway in the days to come. At the center, where the two met in convocation, stood Mount Guyot—the alpine threshold to Summit County and Colorado's rooftop at the Continental Divide. From that vantage, it seemed simply unthinkable that we would be there in less than four days.

---

[8] H. Belloc, *The Path to Rome* (San Francisco: Ignatius Press, 2011), 181.

3

A MOOSE AND HIS PRIESTS

In the early hours of that third morning, we passed in and around the towering granite belfries of the Little Scraggy Mountains. These strange formations felt ancient, and indeed they were, dating back over a billion years. They instilled an inner quiet and awoke in us a sense that we had now entered deeply into the wilderness. By now, the comforts and securities of city life had faded away as distant memory.

"Everything out here is trying to kill us", I heard someone say. The storms were coming, and you could feel it in the air. This signaled the mosquitos to raid, coming in full force to lay siege upon our flesh. We have come to romanticize nature, to think of its pristine form unaffected by the fallenness of things. But the truth had been expressed that day: everything out here really did seem bent on killing us.

The most striking example of this happened several years ago. I was backpacking with two priest friends in a wilderness area known as the Indian Peaks. As evening settled in, we made an altar at the side of a small lake. It was one of those pristine summer evenings, where creation seemed to align with the Eucharistic mystery we were about to celebrate. Having just consecrated bread and wine into the Body and Blood of Christ, I was interrupted mid-sentence: "John, there is a moose behind us... He's out of camp...

No, wait, he is coming right at us!" We turned and froze to look up at the head of a massive bull moose staring right at us from a few feet away. We picked up the paten and chalice and began very slowly to walk away. Then suddenly the moose charged toward us—and stopped, again a few feet away. Attempting to bring panic into submission, we again slowly stepped away—and the moose charged again and stopped. It became patently evident that the "ball was in the moose's court", so to speak; and that this very well might be the end of the priests. But the dance continued until at last we found ourselves in a position to make a run for it. Still carefully holding the Body and Blood of Christ, we went into full sprint and, coming over a hillside, came crashing into a camp of college girls. Mind you, we were still vested as priests (looking like forest-dwelling druids); so when we came violently into their camp, their screams overpowered our attempts to inform them of immanent peril. Fortunately, the moose, satisfied by his assertion of alpha dominance, made for a grove on the other side of the lake—and Holy Mass continued on.

The backcountry is a place where things once again become dangerous. Wild variability is indeed an indispensable ingredient for the making of adventure. It also reminds us of the absolute fragility of human life; for despite the powers and craftiness of man, the wilderness presents circumstances utterly beyond our control. But more importantly, returning to the depths of creation recalls to us a primordial truth, one that is almost entirely lost in our day—the truth of dependence.

Creation is the great school of dependence. Man must depend on both his fellow man and his natural surroundings to survive. This interplay of mutual dependence arises out of the deeper metaphysical reality—that we are all creation. As the *Catechism of the Catholic Church* teaches: "God wills the *interdependence of creatures*. The sun and the moon, the cedar and the little flower, the eagle and the sparrow: the spectacle of their countless diversities and inequalities tells us that no creature is self-sufficient. Creatures exist only in dependence on each other, to complete each other, in the service of each other."[1] One of the great joys of the outdoors is the experience of the interdependence of all things. This, as Giussani writes, leads us back to our very source: "What is most evident immediately following the fact that we exist is that before we lived, we had no life. Therefore, we depend."[2] If man is created and creation is not self-made, then man is intrinsically dependent on the Creator. These are the words of Saint Paul in his famous sermon on Mars Hill: "In him we live and move and have our being" (Acts 17:28).

But just as the Athenians mocked and departed from Saint Paul, so too does modern man scoff at the idea of a relationship of dependence with the Creator God. As Joseph Ratzinger once preached: "Creation is defined as dependence, origin *ab alio* [from another]. Its place is taken by the category of self-creation, which is accomplished through work. Since creation equals dependence, and dependence is the antithesis of freedom, the doctrine of creation is opposed."[3]

For centuries, the groundwork has been laid for a revolution: the supplanting of the Christian vision of creation

---

[1] *Catechism of the Catholic Church*, no. 340.

[2] L. Giussani, *At the Origin of the Christian Claim*, trans. Viviane Hewitt (Montreal: McGill-Queen's University Press, 1998), 85.

[3] J. Ratzinger, *In the Beginning ... A Catholic Understanding of the Story of Creation and the Fall*, trans. Boniface Ramsey, O.P. (Grand Rapids: Eerdmans, 1986), 91.

with the postmodern *ethos* of self-creation. The primary reason for this is the interpretation of dependence as a kind of slavery. Acknowledging myself as creation means I must live with an awareness of my limits; that my life is actually finite and not defined by me. Moreover, to be creation means to depend on another (in fact, *the* Other), a relationship I did not choose. If I seek to disavow this primordial relationship to my Creator, then I must uproot all innate dependence through a total denial of my creatureliness. And this is the path to man's self-destruction.

Christians have a word for this rejection of dependence—sin. At the origin of humanity, an aboriginal catastrophe occurred. In seeking to become gods, man chose to deny his original dependence for the illusion of a total independence. In choosing to live by the lie that we are self-created, we end up rejecting relationality itself. As Ratzinger describes, this is the essence of sin: "They consider their dependence on God's creative love to be an imposition from without."[4]

This rejection of dependence underwent an epochal shift in the Modern era. Its basic framework was called Liberalism, from the Latin *liberare*, "to free". As a philosophy that enshrined man's liberated independence in the form of a holistic worldview, it informed modern political theory and laid the foundations for the American experiment. In this sense, we modern Americans are all "liberals".

What then does Liberalism entail? Man is re-envisioned as an autonomous, self-sustaining being, capable of a totally independent trajectory through the exercise of his reason. These anthropological presuppositions were provided by thinkers such as René Descartes, Jean-Jacques Rousseau, and John Locke. By rethinking the problem, they offered

[4] Ibid., 70.

a new solution; dependence was slavery—and Liberalism, the great emancipator.

Like Transcendentalism, Liberalism is one of the primary components that make up our worldview today. It informs how we think about things far more than we realize. For example, it is commonplace to speak of whether or not one chooses to believe in God. But do we actually get to decide whether God exists? The real question we are asking is whether or not we will depend on God. For the driving conviction of modern man is that his autonomy must determine the course of his life.

Because this purported metaphysical independence is false and unsatisfying, we find ourselves retreating to the depths of creation. Here the great school of dependence recalls to us that we creatures depend on one another because of our shared fundamental dependence on God. Here we re-embrace our total dependence and relearn the primary truth of our humanity. As Ratzinger beautifully summarizes:

> Humans *are* dependent. They cannot live except from others and by trust. But there is nothing degrading about dependence when it takes the form of love, for then it is no longer dependence, the diminishing of self through competition with others. Dependence in the form of love precisely constitutes the self as self and sets it free, because love essentially takes the form of saying, "I want you to be." It is creativity, the only creative power, which can bring forth the other as other without envy or loss of self. Humans are dependent—that is the primary truth about them. And because it is, only love can redeem them, for only love transforms dependence into freedom.... [W]e exist on the foundation of love.[5]

[5] Ibid., 98–99.

In the Incarnation, Jesus Christ is revealed as the "totally relational" man because he was "completely dependent".[6] His secret was the Father. In him the Son finds the unity of personal being, relational dependence, and the infinity of love. Jesus lived without self-deception and a fabricated sense of independence. Being free of isolation, alienation, and autonomy, he was the most fascinating, beautiful, and compelling person ever to walk the earth. In the Redemption, he became an atoning sacrifice for sin and died for our promethean grasp at self-creation. Salvation in Christ arises first in the embrace of our dependence on God, acknowledged as a father and not an abstraction. Only in this can we understand dependence as the very form of filial love and be free of the slavery of independence.

As we arrived at camp that afternoon, a storm broke with great ferocity. We retreated into our tents as the first flashes of lightning and crashes of thunder came. In a mountain storm, one is reminded why the ancients ascribed to the supreme gods of Zeus and Thor the power of thunder. We were simply grateful to be below treeline.

Settling into our 6 × 6 home with my two backcountry roommates, I was reminded of another truth: men usually come to know each other first and then decide if they can depend on each other. But when you are thrown into adventure, the precise opposite happens—you depend on each other and then come to know each other. Such was the case on the trail, which made the evening conversations all the more interesting.

That evening, the conversation shifted to relationships. Not being in the military, I was slow to pick up on

<hr />

[6] Ibid., 75.

the banter. According to Cody, Casey was chasing the "white buffalo", that girl back home who never gave you the time of day; that is, until you returned with combat experience, huge biceps, and a sleeve of tattoos. Casey denied it, and Cody wasn't having it. Things were already escalating, and we were only 10 percent of the way through the trail.

This could be a long month.

4

THE EGO AND THE MOMENT

I had never thought much about tuna, never had an opinion or preference on the matter. But now, staring at my tortilla wrap filled with tuna and goldfish, I began to wonder if I could actually eat this for lunch every day for the next month. And what was more distressing was my digestive tract, which was unresponsive to our trail diet of pure carbohydrates.

Hidden between the small ranges of the Kenosha, South Platte, and Tarryall Mountains is the valley of the Lost Creek. Desirous of the beauty before us, we charged the mountains that morning with renewed vigor. Gaining 3,500 feet, our fifteen-mile trek descended through a citadel of lodgepole pines and, at last, passed into the lush and meadowed valley of the Lost Creek. A perfect home for moose, elk, and bighorn sheep, the beauty of the setting made evident why this place needed to be protected. Lost Creek was the first of six wilderness areas through which we would pass—all of which would provide the trail's most stunning terrain. First established by the Wilderness Act of 1964, the 111 million acres that make up our country's 803 wilderness areas are defined as places untrampled, in which man is permitted to visit but not remain. Indeed, we felt like pilgrims passing through a sanctuary. As our trail turned westward, the mountains again enveloped the hidden valley of the Lost Creek; and there we could see it—the coming of the next storm.

Many people die in the Rocky Mountains every year. Some tragically, by no fault of their own; others by their own volition and drive to push beyond the limits. There were a number of occasions when, by marred judgment and the unabating pursuit of adventure, I should have become another tragic statistic. The first instance of this was in early January of my junior year of high school. Skipping class with a buddy, we made for Grays and Torreys Peaks. We started late, the weather was inclement, and we had never done a winter ascent of a fourteener. Even worse, we only had one pair of crampons and one ice axe between us. As we were traversing the ridge between the peaks, I heard a *snap* and looked back to see my friend's body quickly accelerating down the side of the face. Fortunately, he had the ice axe and after about 500 feet was able to self-arrest, stop the fall, and re-ascend. There I stood alone, just below 14,000 feet, realizing for the first time how perilous my situation was. One wrong step and I too would be heading down the south face of Torreys Peak—without an axe.

Several years later, I read a story of two high school kids who died in that exact same spot on a winter ascent. They, like us, were imprudent and ill-prepared—and tragically did not return from the mountain. Faced with such gravity, I began to ask myself how exactly one can draw the line between the true pursuit of adventure and the recklessness that marked my early days. Though the question is complex and conditioned by circumstance, one thing is certain: whenever the desire for the heights is highjacked by the purposes of the ego, the climber becomes blind and the attempt all the more deadly.

"All that counts is the ego and the moment."[1] These words of Joseph Ratzinger summarized for me the *ethos* of a life ordered and dictated solely by the will to conquer. Within this lay an egotistic drive and relentless pursuit of the moment. It is the self-enclosed modern man, living under the illusion that he is capable of auto-transcendence.

A commonplace but quite helpful word for this is authenticity. No one seems to know how to acquire it, but it is nonetheless instinctively known. In many respects, to be authentic is the last remaining virtue in a world that sees itself as "after virtue". But as we grow older, we look back and see that our drive to be authentic was not much more than the wiles of the ego, grasping at the moment. Even with the best of intentions, we can pursue authenticity *inauthentically*.

When the ego and the moment are untethered from their *telos* (i.e., their purpose and end), they become unintelligible and irreconcilable with our human nature. They also get us in a lot of trouble, even to the point of mortal danger. One of the most classic literary depictions of this is Tolstoy's *Anna Karenina*. In a moment of stirring and intimate intensity, the married woman Anna falls in love with the young Count Vronsky and begins down the path of her own self-destruction. As the tragedy of her life unfolds, Tolstoy concludes: "It showed him [Vronsky] the eternal error people make in imagining that happiness is the realization of desires."[2] Though happiness and the fulfillment of desire are possible, they can never be accomplished if life is conceived as a defiant act of self-creation. Hidden egotism, given to the moment, betrays

---

[1] J. Ratzinger, *The Yes of Jesus Christ: Exercises in Faith, Hope, and Love*, trans. Robert Nowell (New York: Crossroad, 2016), 22.

[2] L. Tolstoy, *Anna Karenina*, trans. Richard Pevear and Larissa Volokhonsky (New York: Penguin Classics, 2004), 37.

man's true desires and razes to the ground his pursuit of a truly authentic life.

In 1933, W.B. Yeats wrote *A Dialogue of Self and Soul* to describe the dialectic between the immortality of the soul and the actualization of the self.[3] It offers a poetic prelude to the philosophical tradition that would enshrine the self's pursuit of authenticity—Existentialism. With Transcendentalism and Liberalism, Existentialism completes the triad of philosophies that make up much of the worldview we bring into the backcountry. Kierkegaard founded Existentialism as a Christian attempt to wrest the individual from the collectivizing menace of Hegelianism. Later, under Nietzsche, Sartre, and Heidegger, Existentialism was secularized and became an anti-Christian call to arms. As Guardini summarized, Existentialism posits the following: "Man is man minus any presuppositions—either essential or ethical. Man is simply free. He must determine himself."[4] What began as an anthropological truth (that man is free and thus a self-determining being) became the sole lens for the interpretation of his existence. It is an approach to life grounded in the idea that there is nothing "given" in man. He has no nature, no essence; his sole aim is to create his own existence through the power of his will. The only way to authenticity is thus to remove the shackles placed upon his freedom—first, his metaphysical dependence on God (and, likewise, the whole Christian tradition) and, then, a subsequent rejection of all relationships. Everything is an imposition on my freedom and must be rejected if I am to be wholly self-made. It is, as Yeats describes, the conquest of the self over the soul, the victory of the ego

[3] Cf. W.B. Yeats, "A Dialogue of Self and Soul", from *The Poems of W.B. Yeats: A New Edition* (New York: Macmillan, 1933), 317–19.

[4] R. Guardini, *The End of the Modern World*, trans. Joseph Theman and Herbert Burke (Wilmington: ISI Books, 1998), 80.

and the promise of the moment. But like all failed anthropologies, Existentialism can only lead to one place—the destruction of man.

If we cannot find the path to authenticity in the self, where then are we to find it? We return to the words of Saint Paul: "Seek the things that are above, where Christ is.... Set your minds on things that are above, not on things that are on earth" (Col 3:1–2). As we make for the heights, we cannot turn inward but must turn upward—to the eternal abode of the Son in the heart of the Father. We cannot find the answer to the question of desire on earth or the capacity for a truly authentic life. As Ratzinger explains, the question of authenticating desire is the basic problem of human existence. "The boundless demands of *eros*, its apparent exaggerations and extravagance, do in reality give expression to a basic problem, indeed *the* basic problem of human existence, insofar as they reflect the nature and intrinsic paradox of love: love demands infinity, indestructibility; indeed, it *is*, so to speak, a call for infinity."[5]

Existentialism got it wrong—we have presuppositions. One of these is the desire for a supernatural destiny. Desire is boundless, only fulfilled in the infinity of love. It can't be removed; it must be followed. And as Giussani writes, this is the very condition for being human.

> Christian religiosity does not spring from a taste for philosophy, but from the dogged insistence of Jesus Christ, who saw in that unique relationship with God the only possibility of safeguarding the value of the individual. Christian religiosity arises as the one and only condition for being human. This is man's choice: either he conceives

[5]J. Ratzinger, *Introduction to Christianity*, trans. J. R. Foster (San Francisco: Ignatius Press, 2004), 302.

of himself as free from the whole universe and dependent only on God, or free from God and therefore the slave of every circumstance.[6]

Only in the humanity of the God-man can my quest for authenticity be authenticated. Following the path of the ego and the moment only ends in the slavery of the circumstance. Either Jesus is the totally authentic man, or the authentic life is categorically impossible. He alone points us to the eternal presupposition of all created being—the Father. At the origin of all things, we find the nuptial union of will and love. Jesus lived authentically because he lived from the Father. These are the existential grounds of the Christian life; that we become authentic, not in ourselves, but in God the Father and through his only begotten Son.

Some choice vocabulary was employed as an immense storm broke upon us. We were exposed in the tributary marshes of Lost Creek and taking a beating. Thunder echoed around us as we finished refilling our water bottles and took off for the woods.

Fortunately, we found the team we sent ahead, sitting in dry tents. All nine of the Fellowship piled into a four-man tent, becoming a small chapel in the sanctuary of the Lost Creek Wilderness. That evening the Son of Man descended in Eucharistic form, drawing our hearts out of the ego and the moment and into the paternal warmth of the Eternal Father.

---

[6] L. Giussani, *At the Origin of the Christian Claim*, trans. Viviane Hewitt (Montreal: McGill-Queen's University Press, 1998), 86.

5

MATHEIN–PATHEIN

The sore limbs and dull wits of haggard men lead to one place—altercations. By the end of our fifth day, we would cover over seventy miles and 10,000 feet of elevation. Our long morning descent out of the Lost Creek Wilderness led us along the lush westward slopes of Kenosha Mountain, later transfigured into rolling aspen groves of the Twin Cone Peaks. Despite the serenity of the terrain, it was clear that we were all hitting a wall.

At midday, I was quietly preparing for Mass near Rock Creek when I heard "Man, I will fight you!" Not surprisingly, these words of acrimony were directed at Cody and Casey. A member of the Fellowship was at a breaking point and ready to fight. Fortunately, he quickly realized that fighting these two G.I.'s was highly inadvisable (plus, Casey had a gun). Eventually things settled and tempers were cooled by the calming words of the Eucharistic Prayer. We were close—only eight miles to Kenosha Pass; but it felt as if the trail were prolonging our arrival. The boys were still pushing, and each step led us closer to our resupply and the conclusion of the trail's first section.

◆ ◆ ◆

Suffering is a distinctively human experience. All animals feel pain; only human beings suffer. Pain is a symptom, informing us that something is wrong in us. Suffering is different—it is a search for the meaningfulness of pain, the *why* of pain. The technological approach, like that of modern medicine, addresses the *cause* of physical or psychological pain, thus attempting to alleviate it. But it cannot answer the question of the *reason* of pain and thereby interpret it. To do this one must enter into the religious sphere, addressing the mysterious origin of things. The *why* of pain requires a different posture, one that is neither clinical nor therapeutic. It is a spiritual question that leads to a profound and countercultural conclusion: "Suffering is not a problem to be solved, but a mystery to be lived."[1]

The Christian proclaims suffering as the way to God. This is utterly remarkable and totally distinctive, a far cry from the Stoic or Buddhist interpretation of suffering. Jesus shows the way to the Father as being *through* the cross, which in essence is the powerlessness of suffering and death. Though it is destined to end in the glory of the Resurrection, suffering remains the way to God. In contrast to this, our postmodern mentality seeks to eliminate the cross and dissolve the question of suffering. But this is titanism, an offense to humanity. The Christian faith invites people, not just to endure suffering, but to interpret it. The Colorado Trail, with its daily ration of physical and mental hardship, brought about a concretely felt experience of suffering. In this way it invited us to consider again the question of its meaning.

The greatest poetic depiction of the Christian vision of suffering comes from Dante's *Divine Comedy*. As Dante and Virgil descend into the cavernous depths of Hell, they pass progressively through its different levels. The first are

---

[1] L. Albacete, *God at the Ritz: Attraction to Infinity* (New York: Crossroad, 2002), 81.

marked by the excessive loves of secondary goods—lust, gluttony, and avarice. The middle of Hell is marked by defective love, namely, sloth. The last three lowest levels of Hell, where the most horrific punishments are to be found, are the places of perverted loves—wrath, envy, and pride. At the very bottom of Hell, we find Satan, frozen in the icy cave of pride, forever consumed by his hatred of the living God.

As they come out on the other side of the world, Dante and Virgil look up and behold the stars. They are escorted to the Isle of Purgatory and begin their ascent up the mountain. Climbing over seven cornices, Dante must be purified of the seven deadly sins—in precisely the reverse order of their descent into Hell. The way of purgation begins with pride and ends with lust. The cornices are steepest at the bottom, gradually easing off until the summit, where we find the celestial Garden of Eden.

Both Hell and Purgatory are places of pain, caused by sin; but the difference between them is that in Purgatory, the pains effect a transformation of the mind. A new consciousness comes to be, a kind of interior awareness that is capable of interpreting suffering as a salvific reality. Led by Virgil, Dante will behold the prideful carrying boulders on their backs, the slothful forced to run, the gluttonous fasting, and the lustful burning in fire. But these pains are not the punishments of divine judgment; they are the penances of divine love. Unless the effects of sin are undone, man is incapable of beginning the celestial ascent of the *Paradiso*. Dante must begin at the bottom, at the gate of Purgatory; there the angel guarding the entrance inscribes seven *P*'s (for *peccatum*, "sin" in Latin) upon his brow with a sword. In the passing of each cornice, one will be removed, until at last, he stands at the summit to behold Beatrice. The ascent is steep and the mountain utterly formidable; but unlike the descent into Hell, with every step of his climb, Dante grows stronger and stronger.[2]

In 2014, the world lost a remarkable priest by the name of Lorenzo Albacete. A native of Puerto Rico and an astrophysicist by training, Albacete was the leader of the ecclesial movement Communion and Liberation. Unassumingly humble and at times outrageous, his witness of Christ centered around his unique personal freedom. He was totally and remarkably himself, absolutely compelling to his secular interlocutors and friends. He wrote a book entitled *God at the Ritz*, which tells of his conversations with the world's elite. In it, he takes up the theme of suffering, beginning with a metaphysical claim: "To be human is to be an incarnate 'why'."[3] Because we are made to ask questions and interpret reality, we must engage suffering as a question and a dialogue with mystery.

As Albacete explains, there are three ways we attempt to eradicate suffering from our lives: (1) by eliminating the source of the pain; (2) by suppressing the question; (3) or by suppressing the self.[4] These attempts to shortcut suffering dehumanize the person, precisely because they secularize it. "The cruelest response to suffering", he writes, "is the attempt to explain it away."[5] In place of this, Christianity offers the truest possible engagement with the reality of suffering. Only by suffering in union with Christ is one able to suffer with others and thereby walk it as a path of transcendence. When suffering is enveloped in the fullness of divine love, it creates the deepest and most powerful experiences of communion with others, one that corresponds to the depths of human desire. Suffering is the

[2] Cf. Dante, *Inferno*, 1:28–30, and *Purgatorio*, 27:121–23.
[3] Albacete, *God at the Ritz*, 86.
[4] Cf. ibid., 85.
[5] Ibid., 102.

birthplace of communion, the place where personhood is drawn out in the experience of sacrificial love. And all of this begins in Jesus Christ, who, sent by the Father, died as an atoning sacrifice of absolute and perfect love.

Before the time of Christ, the Greeks reflected on the theme of suffering according to the axiom *mathein-pathein*. With rhythmic interplay, the two words interpret one another: *mathein*, to learn, and *pathein*, to suffer. To suffer is to learn; to learn is to suffer. All suffering can be a kind of learning; and everything learned must in some way be suffered. In this way, we can see the power and truth of the claim of Christ—the cross is the way to salvation, to intimate knowledge of and loving union with God. But the cross is the experience of powerlessness unto death. This is why we abhor it and seek to eliminate it. But what happens when we suppress the suffering heart? Man loses God, and even himself. For even the Son of God was not exempt from this in his human nature; as Saint Paul tells us, "although he was a Son, he learned (*mathein*) obedience through what he suffered (*pathein*)" (Heb 5:8).

So, we return time and again to the mountains to suffer. These great educators of creaturehood, offering pain to the body and hardship to the soul, give something so much greater—they reawaken the heart to the *why* of suffering.

Before us now was the most expansive and breathtaking vista we had yet seen. As the trail headed northbound to the pass, we beheld the South Park—a grassland flat situated at 10,000 feet, the largest in the state. Enclosed as a basin between the Continental Divide in the north, Mosquito Range to the west, its thousand square miles are centered upon the town of Fairplay. From our vantage point, we could look beyond the Park and see the Collegiate

Peaks—those soaring majesties that we would be traversing in the coming days.

We had met strange characters on the trail, but none as unrepeatable as those who agreed to meet us at resupply points. The first of these was Todd, a quixotic evangelical who awaited us with banter, whiskey, and theological interrogation. We bid farewell to the Fellowship and spent the evening moving toward what the Thomistic tradition calls "the point of *hilaritas*". The first multi-day section was finished, but six remained. The night was joyous and festive, but we knew what was coming. We were only five days in and still had hundreds of miles to go. Tomorrow we would leave the beautiful South Park and ascend beyond the treeline and unto the towering heights of the Continental Divide.

6

IN THAT PURE AIR

The sixth day on the trail was one of great anticipation. Now, just 2,700 feet above us stood the rooftop of America—the Continental Divide. Once we reached this point, we would spend the next 235 miles either upon it or near it, conjoined with what is known as the Continental Divide Trail (which spans 3,000 miles from Canada and Mexico). The vistas we had known to this point were mere hints and guesses of what our eyes would behold in the coming days.

Setting off from Kenosha Pass, we gradually traversed the aspen-lined borderlands of the South Park before hitting our inevitable, vertical challenge. Though our daily portion was only 11.6 miles, all the elevation was to come in the last two miles. With the rising trail, the heat intensified, as did our fatigue. Every turn through the forested switchbacks gave a false promise of the end, until at last we stepped out above the treeline—that haunted frontier where all living things seem to vanish in the oxygen-depleted air.

Looking far up a protracted and verdant alpine meadow, we saw Georgia Pass; our meeting point with the Divide, entryway into Summit County, and, most consolingly, our campsite for the night. A half mile up the meadow, a large black spot stood in stark contrast to the purity of its green surroundings. Cody, with hunter's pride, claimed it was a black bear. Casey detracted, called it a bush. Both offended by the other's judgment, they shook on it and made the first of the trail's many "beer bets". We would soon zag through the meadow and, within half an hour, meet our foe—a bear or a bush.

In my years in the Colorado backcountry, I have been blessed with the companionship of good friends. But when I moved to Italy for graduate studies, things changed. Now living in a strange land where I knew no one and could barely speak the language, I found myself, for the first time, alone. During that first summer, I took off on an adventure, hiking on the Gran Paradiso of the Graian Alps. That night I returned to the hut, and, after a failed attempt at common room comradery, I went back to my bunk and picked up the *Letters* of Pier Giorgio Frassati (d. 1925). This young Italian climber, beatified by the Church for his heroic sanctity, was in many respects my only friend in the country. I opened the book at random, read the first letter, and almost dropped the book out of shock. At the bottom of the page, just beneath the signature, Pier Giorgio wrote the place where he was—Rifugio Vittorio Sella—the exact hut I was in. It was a moment of invisible communion and indescribable intimacy. It recalled to me something I had forgotten: that because God is himself a relationship, all who are in him are in relationship. I then returned to Frassati's words with fresh perspective: "Every day I fall in love with the mountains more and more, and if my studies would allow me to do it, I would spend entire days on the mountains contemplating in that pure air the Greatness of the Creator."[1]

---

[1] P. G. Frassati, *Letters to His Friends and Family*, trans. Timothy E. Deeter (Ann Arbor: Alba House, 2009), 132.

Being in relationship with the living God was the secret to Frassati's contemplation. He understood that the creation he beheld spoke of relationship. This stands in radical contrast to modern man, who no longer speaks of creation but of "nature". This subtle shift in language reveals a deeper metaphysical change: we now think of the world as the a-personal, self-subsisting atmosphere of our lives. As Romano Guardini elaborates:

> Here the consciousness of the believer must make a fundamental distinction: the world is not Nature, but Creation, creation in the plain sense of a work brought forth by a free act. It is not something "natural", self-evident, self-justified, but it requires a reason, and it is given this reason by the power which created it in its being and reality.... To put it another way: the world does not have to be, but it is, because it was created. The act by which it was created did not need to take place, but it took place because it was willed. It might not have been willed, but it was willed because it was willed. This means that the world is not a necessity, but a fact. This is the distinguishing characteristic of the Biblical view of existence: the world is based upon an act.[2]

To be created means to come from the freedom of another. In this way, all of creation is first and foremost relational. But as moderns, we deny this basic truth, thinking of ourselves first as individuals and only secondly in relationship. In doing this, we eclipse the givenness of our lives and deny our primordial relationship. As "a being that did not make myself", I am either a random event of chance or a pure gift of love. If the latter is true, then the giver of the gift must be a relationship that defines everything.

[2] R. Guardini, *The World and the Person*, trans. Stella Lange (Chicago: Henry Regnery, 1965), 255.

Having spent a lot of time in picturesque mountain towns, I have often wondered why they contain such escalated levels of drug abuse and suicide. It seems to me that the intense proximity to creation, itself calling for relationship, makes the denial of God and the experience of loneliness all the more unbearable. The drama of good and evil always plays out in the arena of relationship, both divine and human. As Ratzinger explains, it is here that we find the fundamental pattern of human existence.

> Human beings are relational, and they possess their lives— themselves—only by way of relationship. I alone am not myself, but only in and with you am I myself. To be truly a human being means to be related in love, to be *of* and *for*. But sin means the damaging or the destruction of relationality. Sin is a rejection of relationality because it wants to make the human being a god.[3]

The relational logic of humanity, and in fact all of creation, is twofold.

First, it is Trinitarian. God is one being in three persons, a perfect relationship and eternal exchange of love. God's perfection lies in his totalizing relationships. For as Saint Thomas Aquinas so powerfully concluded, in God the persons do not have relationships, they *themselves* are the relations (person = *relatio subsistens*).[4] The unity of person and relation in God reveals the essential call of the created, human person: *to be perfect is to be nothing other than relation.* How radically different this vision of perfection is!

Second, this relational logic is *perichoretic*. This ancient term, literally meaning "to dance around", was used by

[3] J. Ratzinger, *In the Beginning ... A Catholic Understanding of the Story of Creation and the Fall*, trans. Boniface Ramsey, O.P. (Grand Rapids: Eerdmans, 1986), 72–73.

[4] Thomas Aquinas, *Summa Theologiae*, I, q. 29, a. 4.

the Church Fathers to describe a deeper insight into the
way the Divine Persons relate. They are not separate and
isolated in the Godhead, but are in such intimate and close
relationship that they mutually indwell and interpene-
trate one another. While remaining themselves, they are
immersed in the others. A beautiful created image of this
is marriage: when man and woman enter into the covenant of matrimony, the two become one flesh—a single
mystery of two persons who are no longer separate individuals. This one relationship now defines everything that
they are. At the depths of the experience of love, "when
we love a person and long for a return of our love, it is the
heart of the other person which we want to call ours."[5] All
loves speak of the perichoretic mystery of God's interpersonal love: "I am in the Father and the Father is in me ...
[and] you will know that I am in my Father, *and you in me
and I in you*" (Jn 14:11–20; emphasis added).

My time alone in the *Rifugio Vittorio Sella* was a reminder
that companionship is *the* essence of life because God is *the*
relationship of love. We need others to reflect back to us
this mystery within ourselves. But if we were to do so apart
from God, we would find ourselves only in the disori-
enting perplexity of a hall of mirrors—images in constant
reflection, yet not in reality. True friends beckon us out
of the prisons of our egos, awakening us to the real. For it
is not "ideas, discourses, and logic" that change a person,
writes Giussani, but only "being together with others".[6]

We were exhausted and grateful to reach Georgia Pass at
last. Beneath the imposing tower of Mount Guyot, we

---

[5] D. von Hildebrand, *The Heart* (South Bend: St. Augustine's Press, 2007), 67.

[6] L. Giussani, S. Alberto, and J. Prades, *Generating Traces in the History of the World: New Traces in the Christian Experience*, trans. Patrick Stevenson (Montreal: McGill-Queen's University Press, 2010), 51.

breathed in the pure air of the Continental Divide. We stood upon this "Great Wall" of the American West with a sense of triumph and relief.

In truth, all triumph and relief were Casey's that night. There had been no bear, and he had won his first beer. But in Cody's defense, we agreed it was the fiercest looking shrubbery any of us had ever seen.

7

LOST IN THE COSMOS

Climbing out of a frosted tent, we took our morning coffee with the regimented silence of men not yet prepared for sociality. The feeling of an alien cold, one proper to life above treeline, hung on as we started our short hike to Georgia Pass. Upon our arrival, we were surprised to find a random collective of individuals enjoying a sunrise breakfast. Cody informed me that this was called a *tramily*, or "trail family".

Cody had seen many of these trail families when he hiked the Pacific Crest. In his typical silent fashion, he made it clear that we would not be joining them. In the weeks to come, we would encounter a number of these groups. In truth, they were a little strange; for more than the libertine *esprit* of a nomadic life is required to make a family. What we thru-hikers intended was something nobler, something that could be called Christian community.

"Men of Athens, I perceive that in every way you are very religious", Saint Paul begins in his speech on the Areopagus. "What therefore you worship as unknown," he continued, "I proclaim to you" (Acts 17:22–23). Despite the evangelistic failure of Paul's Areopagitic *kerygma*, we see once again how deeply religious the ancient pagan mind was. Atheism, in its modern, metaphysical form, was simply unthinkable and, contrary to popular belief, did not exist in the pre-Christian world.

Nowadays the Areopagus is inverted. The Christian evangelist first perceives his contemporary as non-religious; they are not only *not* worshipping the *unknown God* (of the pagan), they have rejected the *known God* (of the Christian). It is simply false to think of atheism as a neutral religious standpoint; it is in fact composed of rejection of the Christian claim. In this way, von Balthasar concludes, "atheism is a specifically post-Christian phenomenon."[1]

One hike in particular brought this to my attention. I had met a young Dominican Sister in Denver, who, after begging me for months, finally persuaded me to take her and her Sisters on an elementary fourteener known as Mount Democrat. Sympathetic that they were hiking in full religious habit, I wore clerics (the first and last time I would do this). We were quite the sight arriving at the summit—four religious Sisters and a priest—looking as if we had taken a wrong turn out of the Renaissance Festival. The interactions ranged throughout the full gambit of human experience: the innocent, yet obnoxious stares of the utterly stunned, the cold and hardened looks of the disenchanted, those enthused by a circus affair—and lastly, a few remnant Christians who found quiet yet profound delight in joining us for Mass. Such was the state of our world, revealed in a new way on the mountaintop.

The situation of modern atheism is more dire than ever before. It is not the denial of God that is concerning; it is that the God-question is nearly irrelevant. In another way,

---

[1] H. U. von Balthasar, "Spirit and Fire: An Interview with Hans Urs von Balthasar", in *Communio* 32 (Fall 2005): 577.

we could say that God is being "un-thought". Modern
man has convinced himself that he is too busy and distracted to think on the things of God. But the reality is
harsher: because the notion of God has no bearing on life,
the question becomes almost unthinkable. Three centuries
ago, atheists were bellicose and passionately anti-Christian.
They denied everything, but at least they cared. In our
day, the bold fideism of the atheist has collapsed into the
fatigued apathy of the agnostic.

This is evidenced by the rising phenomenon of the
postmodern *none*, of which we spoke earlier. At present,
25 percent of Americans profess to being nones, up from
6 percent in the early 1990s. One in every five cradle-
Catholics are now nones (not just lapsed but disaffiliated).
And this number is accelerating: the percentage of nones
under the age of thirty is 40 percent.[2] We are witnessing
the drastic effects of secularization, finally coming to fru-
ition in our technocratic age. As Guardini saw so clearly
a century before: "Man has now grown up and become
adult and 'God' is simply the obstacle on the path to complete self-realization."[3] Church pews have grown cold as
the postmodern none sets out on the trail of self-discovery,
in the company, not of the Church, but of the tramily.

Of all people, Friedrich Nietzsche speaks a prophetic
word to the postmodern none; that though you have
abandoned the God-question, you are still lost to yourself. "We are unknown, we knowers, to ourselves.... Of
necessity we remain strangers to ourselves, we understand
ourselves not, in our selves we are bound to be mistaken,
for each of us holds good to all eternity the motto, 'Each

---

[2] Cf. S. Bullivant, *Mass Exodus: Catholic Disaffiliation in Britain and America since Vatican II* (Oxford: Oxford University Press, 2019), 244.

[3] R. Guardini, *Freedom, Grace, and Destiny: Three Chapters in the Interpretation of Existence*, trans. John Murray, S.J. (New York: Pantheon Books, 1961), 87.

is the farthest away from himself'—as far as ourselves are concerned we are not knowers."[4] The self is displaced. We don't know where and who we are. In response to this, the satirical genius Walker Percy penned *Lost in the Cosmos: The Last Self-Help Book*. To illustrate our misplaced egos, he posed the following question: "Why is it that, when you are shown a group photograph in which you are present, you always (and probably covertly) seek yourself out?"[5] He caught us, once again, looking at our ourselves. Is it just vanity? No, he writes—you are just looking for yourself.

Even if we relegate the God-question to the sphere of irrelevance, we cannot *not* try to make sense of our being in the cosmos. In the phenomenon of the postmodern none, we see a worldview that is uncritically assimilated. No wonder his levels of anxiety are the highest in recorded history—he is attempting to dismantle the structure of human existence all with feigned ignorance and self-assertive skepticism. But Nietzsche remains a prophet: no matter how many mountains you climb and how many thru-hikes you have packed, you are tortured by the fact that you don't know who and what you are. As Percy writes from the Christian perspective:

> With the passing of the cosmological myths and the fading of Christianity as a guarantor of the identity of the self, the self becomes dislocated ... is both cut loose and imprisoned by its own freedom, yet imprisoned by a curious and paradoxical bondage like a Chinese handcuff, so that the very attempts to free itself, e.g., by ever more refined techniques for the pursuit of happiness, only tighten the

[4] F. Nietzsche as quoted on the title page of W. Percy, *Lost in the Cosmos: The Last Self-Help Book* (New York: Picador, 2000).
[5] Ibid., 7.

bondage and distance the self ever farther from the very world it wishes to inhabit as its homeland.[6]

With Percy, we stumble upon the key—that the loss of God is intimately connected to the loss of man. As Léon Bloy wrote, "where there is no God, there is no man either."[7] We are made, not for skeptical disregard, but for the passionate pursuit of truth. Our own self-interpretation is bound up with our innate desire to become aware of reality and adhere properly to it. In the beautiful insight of Saint John Henry Newman:

> Resolve to believe nothing, and you must prove your proofs and analyze your elements, sinking farther and farther, and finding "in the lowest depth a lower depth," till you come to the broad bosom of scepticism. I would rather be bound to defend the reasonableness of assuming that Christianity is true, than to demonstrate a moral governance from the physical world. Life is for action. If we insist on proofs for every thing, we shall never come to action: to act you must assume, and that assumption is faith.[8]

Only by making relevant the God question can man begin again to pursue the answer to his existence. Only then can we be free of existential irritation and the impetuosity of a self, unnerved by its own displacement. But the God-question is only truly relevant when concretized in the person and life of Jesus Christ. Without him, God is an abstraction, the one Nietzsche pronounced dead. When

[6] Ibid., 12–13.

[7] L. Bloy as quoted in H. de Lubac, *The Drama of Atheist Humanism*, trans. Edith M. Riley, Anne Englund Nash, and Mark Sebanc (San Francisco: Ignatius Press, 1995), 65.

[8] J. H. Newman, *An Essay in Aid of a Grammar of Assent* (South Bend: University of Notre Dame Press, 1979), 91.

Christianity is experienced as an event, the God-question resurrects to new life. In the historical fact of Jesus, we are given again the path to God.

Descending from the Continental Divide and back into forested highlands, the trail started to feel monotonous. Despite the subtle beauty of Keystone Mountain's forested glades, it was our seventh day, and we were tired of trees. We then saw a sign of hope: white rocks beside the trail in the shape of "100". We had reached mile 100 of the trail and gained the first 17,000 feet of elevation. This brought relief and enough sense of accomplishment to bring us to the next day.

But our celebration was cut short by the onslaught of yet another storm. It hurried us into an unsuspecting meadow, whose gruff surface provided a rather undesirable bed. We retired early and permitted the restless thoughts of a tiresome day to dissolve into the alpine dreams of a new day to come.

8

THE BEGINNING OF MANHOOD

I stumbled about my sleeping bag looking for my head-lamp. It was 2 a.m., and I was sedated by poor sleep and a sense of impending dread. Then I heard the quiet, enchanting voice of Ray Charles—Casey was playing "America the Beautiful". That sultry organ awakened me from my interior monologue, recalling the sentiments and memories of my American childhood. It was the Fourth of July.

We had talked for several days about day 8, which we deemed "the barnburner". Eighteen miles and 4,400 feet of elevation to gain stood between us and our first break day at the resort town of Copper Mountain. But there was a problem, or rather an obstacle: in the middle of our western march was a mountain range known as the Ten-mile. We would gain 3,000 feet in the first eight miles, then, cresting the range at a pass, begin the long descent to town.

At about 3:30 in the morning, passing through wooded slopes north of the town of Breckenridge, we suddenly froze—for through the pitch black of that dark night, two glowing, green eyes stared at us from just beside the trail.

"Mountain lion", whispered Casey. And before he finished saying the word, his handgun was out of the holster, cocked, and ready to fire. Time froze within the stare of those green eyes. Then suddenly the showdown began as the animal quickly darted in the opposite direction. Before the shot was fired, our lamps shown on the predator, revealing, not a mountain lion, but a mule deer. Casey had nearly killed Bambi.

As the adrenaline subsided, we remembered why Casey carried a gun and was tempted to shoot anything that threatened us in the dark. Several years ago, he had been hiking Mount Elbert, solo and unarmed. As he descended down the side of the peak, he realized something was haunting his steps. It was a mountain lion, stalking his prey. As any Coloradan knows, there is nothing more terrifying. Typically, by the time you see the predator, it's too late. Fortunately for Casey, he survived the chase and made it back to his car. But from then on, he was always armed and ready at night.

We hit the base of the Tenmile peaks at sunrise and decided that war paint was in order. We prepared for battle during that intense chill that hits you just before dawn. As painted men, we began our assault on the heights of the ancient Gore Fault, a major line that uplifted during the time of the Ancestral Rockies (circa 300 million years ago). As we hit treeline and the sun hit us, the vistas opened anew to the wild brilliance of the alpenglow on the high peaks.

The barnburner of the Tenmile Range brought about the question of limitations. Along with dependence and relationality, limitations are the third aspect of our creatureliness—a third key to understanding what it means to be created. We can think of limitations in two ways: mental/physical limitations and metaphysical limitations.

As a child, I remember my dad teaching us about limitations. He learned all about them in Ranger School. "Boys," he would often say to my brother and me, "remember that you can push your body so much farther than your mind tells you that you can. Don't be afraid to push beyond the limitations of what you think you have." What my dad taught us from experience has been confirmed by physiological research. Paradigms have shifted as we have come to realize that the limitations of the body are in fact "curiously elastic".[1] The mysterious power of the human will is capable of far more than the mind limits itself to believe. In short, there is always more, and we can always go farther. In a particular way, it is the role of the father to educate his children in understanding their limitations. This means teaching them, like my dad did, to have *grit*, push hard when one must, and never surrender to the appearance of limitations.

But there is a deeper kind of limitation, one greater than the relationship of the mind and body. This we call *metaphysical* limitations, a kind of limit upon us (not within us). These limits imply that at the very depths of our being, we are finite, defined, and, in fact, limited in our abilities. The most significant boundaries are the facts that we were born and will die and that everything in between is defined by time and space. In this sense, there is only so much you can do in your life, only so much your spiritual and physical being can endure. We are not limitless, as much as the experience of transcending limits may give us a sense of that. In this way, man is a walking paradox: he must simultaneously push beyond the physical limits in order to explore the full potentiality of his nature, all the while surrendering to the metaphysical limitations that define his very created being.

Just as the father is the one who teaches us how to push physically beyond our limitations, he must educate

---

[1] Cf. A. Hutchinson, *Endure: Mind, Body and the Curiously Elastic Limits of Human Performance* (New York: HarperCollins, 2018).

us in learning to embrace our metaphysical limitations. The latter is perhaps the most important step into true manhood: only a father can help us understand our limitations and find meaning in them. For in the embrace of his own limits, a father points to the fatherhood of God. Truly limitless, God the Father is the origin and source of all fatherhood. In the eternal exchange of infinite love, the Father sent his limitless, divine Son to assume the limitations of creation and, thus, reconcile all creation to the Father. The entire vision of Christian redemption centers upon this: the limitlessness of paternal love in the Son of God redeems man precisely from within his limited, finite being. Jesus accomplishes this through his self-giving love on the Cross, becoming poor that we may be rich (cf. 2 Cor 8:9). As limitations render us poor, the inner logic of surrender emerges as the form of the gift of self. "Everything depends on this poverty towards God," von Balthasar concludes, "and in God, poverty of God in us."[2] Herein lies the beginning of manhood.

But in a fatherless age such as our own, it is difficult to transcend the perpetuating adolescence of men and women who reject their limitations. Ratzinger finds this to be part and parcel of sin: "At the very heart of sin lies human beings' denial of their creatureliness, inasmuch as they refuse to accept the standard and the limitations that are implicit in it. They do not want to be creatures, do not want to be subject to a standard, do not want to be dependent."[3]

Limitations denote standards, the way things are measured. It is titanism to attempt otherwise. And this titanic

[2] H. U. von Balthasar, *Science, Religion, and Christianity*, trans. Hilda Graef (London: Burns and Oates, 1958), 102.

[3] J. Ratzinger, *In the Beginning ... A Catholic Understanding of the Story of Creation and the Fall*, trans. Boniface Ramsey, O.P. (Grand Rapids: Eerdmans, 1986), 70.

drive within us reveals both our desire to be godlike as well as an insatiable draw to limitlessness. Only in Christ, the Son of the Father, can we find the paradoxical balance of pushing the limits of our physio-moral life, all the while more deeply embracing the metaphysical limits of our being. Much of the contemporary outdoor milieu a priori rejects this paradox; and in refusing to acknowledge limitations, ends up in the catastrophes of alpine fatality. "Man today holds power over things," Guardini writes, "but we can assert confidently that he does not yet have power over his own power."[4]

Man's struggle with limitations is powerfully expressed in the ancient story of Odysseus. After ten years fighting in the Trojan War, Homer's epic tells the adventure of Odysseus' journey home—his *Odyssey*. The story ends with the reconquest of his home kingdom of Ithaca and the reunion with his Queen Penelope. Centuries later, Dante continues the story with creative liberty. Rather than seeing him as a heroic warrior whose life ends peacefully at home, he describes him as a restless wanderer, who can't stay at Ithaca for long. Heading out into the forbidden waters of the West, he passes the Straits of Gibraltar in search of the Isle Mount of Purgatory. Just as he gains sight of the mountain, his ship capsizes, and he drowns. In Canto 26 of the *Inferno*, Dante and Virgil find him in the depths of Hell, where he tells the story of his restless pursuit. As he describes, it was his slavish yielding to the endless thrill and pursuit of adventure that ended his life so tragically. In Odysseus, Dante provides an enduring lesson to all of us who seek the heights and the depths—that limitations will always have the final word.

---

[4] R. Guardini, *The End of the Modern World*, trans. Joseph Theman and Herbert Burke (Wilmington: ISI Books, 1998), 90.

I remember the day I learned that I had metaphysical limitations. While I was living in Europe, I had the opportunity to climb "the mountain of mountains"—the Matterhorn. Arriving at the *Hörlihütte*, my climbing partner and our guides prepared to climb the northeast ridge toward the summit. It was the feast of Our Lady of the Snows (August 5th), and when I found out that it was the patronal feast of the local town, I took it as a sign that our venture would be a success. Then it snowed—all night—and we awoke long before dawn faced with a crucial decision as to whether we would attempt the summit. Six inches of snow covered several inches of *verglas* (a transparent, glazed ice) on the rocky face. Additionally, two British climbers had frozen to death on the ridge that night. My climbing partner and our guides put the question to me, advising against the climb but admitting their willingness. In that moment, I realized the metaphysical limits around my dream to climb the Matterhorn; I embraced them, possibly for the first time, and said, "No, we won't climb." In the midst of my shattered dream and intense disappointment, I felt a deep and powerful spiritual peace. I knew in that moment that I would likely never have the opportunity to climb the Matterhorn—and that that was OK. I had already had several days of exceptional alpinism, summiting peaks like the *Dufour-spitze* and the *Breithorn*—peaks no one knew and by which no one would be impressed back home. But limits are limits, and when they arise out of the metaphysical contours of our created being, we must reverence them with a religious submission of mind and heart.

High up on the Tenmile Range, we could now see the pass. Seeing mountain bikers on the trail above us, we set our task to catch them and beat them to the top. This was the moment I realized we had become savages—we were trying to chase down people on bicycles. At last we gained the heights where we celebrated and offered Mass (still in the war paint). We had reached the summit of the Tenmile Range before the coming of the afternoon storms—and we basked in a luminous communion of sunlight, accomplishment, and gratitude to God.

But we were not done. We knew that the descent would be steep and that our knees would start to go. And it was far more grueling and much longer than expected. At last we made it to the road, thinking we were just a few minutes from the resort of Copper Mountain, our place of refuge and rest. But it was still a few miles away, and things got *stormy* (both monsoonal rains and interpersonal relationships). We trudged along, harboring a grudge against the landscape. In a moment of desperation and utter brilliance, Cody dropped his pack and took off in full sprint. Chasing down a cart lady from the local golf course, he returned with a round of beers. In our eyes, Jason had just returned with the golden fleece. And as we walked into the village of Copper Mountain, we indeed felt like argonauts. Through crowds of tourists walked a pack of men in war paint, with the crazed look of castaways in their eyes; men who had just covered 120 miles over four mountain ranges in eight days; men who with beers in hand, sang and cheered to the theme song of *The Magnificent Seven*. As a staring crowd fell silent, we sat down to the patio bar. People fled as the rain started to pour once again. But we remained. At this point we had passed through it all. It was a moment of unspeakable joy. We had made it to our first break day. And with the hidden smiles of quixotic, exhausted men, we hoisted another round—and toasted our limitations.

9

ANIMA TECHNICA VACUA

We woke late to the sound of rain pounding on the resort town of Copper Mountain. We started the day at a lethargic pace, which felt strange after so many consecutive alpine starts. When on the trail, each morning on the trail was charged with adrenaline; we always woke long before dawn and set our task to the day's mission. But today, our first of two break days off the trail, felt strange and restless. We woke late to find ourselves trapped in a bizarre place. Copper Mountain, a hybrid of alpine retreat and outdoor amusement park, was filled with the noise and frenzy of American tourism.

Late that morning, Luke arrived. He was to be the fourth and last of the thru-hikers joining Cody, Casey, and myself. I had met Luke nine months prior and knew immediately that he was the kind of man I wanted on the trail. A Texas-born college football player, Luke's presence and bearing carried a clear-cut intensity as defined as his jawline. At first impression, he could be taken for a bionic man. But he was, like Cody and Casey, a real man—self-possession, matched with naturalness and an ability to endure hardship. I knew he would complement and round out the team, saving us from the savage devolution to which, if left to ourselves, we would likely succumb.

But Cody and Casey were not convinced. Over lunch, Luke sat trial, as this duo of military force conducted their silent interrogation. The pouring rain outside made me wonder if they were going to waterboard him. But Luke remained cool-handed. Apparently, I was the only one unnerved by the standoff, plagued with doubts that my election of such diverse characters would not come together in the team I needed. But only time would tell.

Despite the restless awkwardness of the break day, it provided a touchpoint back to the modern world. I saw anew the stark contrast between the backcountry and the urbanized village in which we found ourselves. Most specifically, we had been reintroduced to technology—to that transformative power that had come to dominate, and ultimately manipulate, the human experience.

Now technology is not bad in itself. Several years prior, I was on a backcountry ski trip in a hut not far from Copper Mountain. On the first morning, I woke with unspeakable tooth pain. Here we were in the middle of nowhere, just above 11,000 feet, in winter—and I needed a root canal. With no chance of escape for three days, I had no option but to endure it and drink as much whiskey as possible. So ended my usual diatribe, musing on the glories of the pre-industrial world. It was an arresting realization that modern life afforded exceptional comforts for the alleviation of suffering—and that I was in fact no way ready to be separated from them.

When the ancient Greeks invented the word *technē* (the etymological root of "technology"), they meant something very different from how we understand it. Originally, the term meant "art" or "craft" and covered most activities in which man engaged in order to form nature to his designs. This is likewise where we get the word "technique", the skill by which something is done. *Technē* was, for Plato and Aristotle, to be matched with another uniquely human activity—*epistēmē*, or "knowledge". The highest form of *technē* (art), matched with the highest form of *epistēmē* (philosophy), was the summit of Hellenistic culture and an indispensable foundation for Western civilization.

With the birth of modernity, *technē* took on an entirely new meaning. In place of an art form of man's creative intuition, it was transformed into a desire to master and manipulate nature. This philosophical shift first occurred in the revolutionary ideas of men like Francis Bacon and René Descartes. When the vision of man had changed, so too the meaning of his actions upon nature. The world was to be "technologized" according to this new approach to reality, and this happened in two ways. First, we saw it in the form of industrialization. Through the advances derived from the scientific method, we conceived of new mechanics unleashing unthinkable powers in the way of economic production. Thus, an industrial revolution was born. Throughout the eighteenth and nineteenth centuries, this revolution caused a secondary effect of an urbanization of the world. People left their centuries-old agrarian life and moved to cities to work in factories. The effects of this were humanly devastating; not simply because of the abysmal circumstances of the new workplace, but because of the total estrangement of man from his natural habitat in creation. But in the last century, a second technological revolution unfolded. For these industrial advances made way for an entirely new mode of technology—the coming digitalization of the world. This is technology as we now speak of it, the creation of a virtual reality that is increasingly becoming the place of all human experience. At present, the average person spends eleven hours and six

minutes a day using digital media—an astonishing statistic
with truly unrealized ramifications.[1]

I first began thinking about the inherent consequences
of our technological society on a trip to southern Colorado. At the bottom of the Sangre de Cristo Mountains,
tucked away between three mountain giants, lies Lake
Como. To get to this tiny, pristine locale, one must either
trudge a fourteen-mile approach from the desert plain
below—or get a ride up the most gnarly and death-defying
four-wheel drive trail in the state. The road to Lake Como
is incredibly perilous; at three points (known as Jaws #1,
#2, and #3), you see memorial placards of those who died
attempting the drive.

But arriving at the lake, you see that nothing is partic-
ularly remarkable (apart from the name). It was here that
I opened the book *Letters from Lake Como* by Romano
Guardini, a powerful testimony against the industrialization of modern Europe. Growing up in southern Germany, Romano Guardini returned to his birthplace in the
Lake Como region of Northern Italy and was astonished
at what he found. The beautiful backdrop of century-old
alpine villages was now dominated by the smug ugliness
of factories. He, like Tolkien in the north of England,
deplored the conquest of the natural surroundings and its
irreparable consequences. His letters, written in the 1920s,
laid the first groundwork for his lifetime project of interpreting the consequences of modern, technological society in a post-Christian world. The ancient lake of Como
attested to the delayed yet inevitable victory of modernity
over both the classical and Christian culture that for nearly
two millennia had serenely abided within it. As Guardini
would write: "When I came to Italy the question became

[1] M. Easter, *The Comfort Crisis: Embrace Discomfort to Reclaim Your Wild,
Happy, Healthy Self* (New York: Rodale Books, 2021), 193.

very severe. All its beauty filled me with sorrow.... I saw
machines invading the land that had previously been the
home of culture. I saw death overtaking a life of infinite
beauty, and I felt that this was not just an external loss that
we could accept and remain who we were."[2]

Even before the advent of the digital, Guardini perceived
the spirit of technological domination as anti-human and
anti-culture. The uninhibited and unquenchable thirst for
the conquest of nature was now coming to dominate man
himself. Guardini began to unmask the deeper truths of
this modern project. He describes this domination in three
ways: mastery, abstraction, and the artificiality of existence.
These three technological modes were laying the grounds
of an "alternate universe, self-sufficient, and almost independent of *given* nature."[3]

As a student of Romano Guardini, Hans Urs von Balthasar assumed his call to arms in acknowledging the destruc-
tive quietude of modern, technological advancement. He
coined a unique phrase, and as is common to his style,
dropped it like a microphone at the end of his *magnus opus*.
"But where is the famous 'point of contact' with the *anima
technica vacua*. I for one certainly do not know. Some table-
rapping, a séance or two, some dabbling in Zen meditation, a smattering of liberation theology: enough."[4]

What von Balthasar signals for us here is not just the
advances of technology on the natural realm, but its invasion, and indeed transformation, of the spiritual life of
man. His phrase *anima technica vacua* is translated as "vac-
uous, technological soul". Prior to modernity, the soul of
the West was Christian, a worldview providing it with

[2] R. Guardini, *Letters from Lake Como: Explorations in Technology and the Human
Race*, trans. Geoffrey W. Bromiley (Grand Rapids: Eerdmans, 1994), 4–5.

[3] L. Dupré, "Introduction", in Guardini, *Letters from Lake Como*, viii–xiv.

[4] H. U. von Balthasar, *Epilogue*, trans. Edward T. Oakes (San Francisco:
Ignatius Press, 2005), 11.

a unique, spiritual unity. According to this view, man's spiritual quest to interpret reality was ordered to God and thereby afforded him a harmonious communion with nature. Nowadays, the *anima technica vacua* has displaced this Christian vision: trustful surrender is supplanted by the spirit of mastery; the reality of things in themselves dissolved into mental abstraction; and the natural, being eclipsed by an artificially constructed universe, is leading toward a singular goal: the titanic attempt of self-creation and a final, divine enthronement of the ego of man.

We might leave the city and go into nature—but we carry into it our technological mentality. Unless we embrace God as the source of all things, we will bring our techno-activism, psychedelics, and our world-denying spirituality with us wherever we are. It is the new *anima* of man's new spiritual life, one that is helpless against the onslaught of the machines. As von Balthasar writes: "Everyone realizes that we cannot go 'back to nature,' as Rousseau naively imagined, nor shut our eyes, as the romantics did.... We have to find a mode of living with the monsters so that man can control them, and enforce his superiority to the robots, though it is certain to be an exacting task ... no machine has ever made the slightest contribution to prayer."[5]

Christians have always left the city, but for a deeper reason: to encounter the living God in the posture of authentic Christian prayer. This prayer arises out of the primary realization that our home is not in this world— that we are in fact pilgrims. "For here we have no lasting city, but we seek the city which is to come" (Heb 13:14). As Saint Augustine so powerfully noted, it was Cain, not Abel, who founded the first city, later to become the great

---

[5] H. U. von Balthasar, *Science, Religion, and Christianity*, trans. Hilda Graef (London: Burns and Oates, 1958), 55.

city of Babel. This city he calls "the City of Man", which stands in contrast to "the City of God". For Augustine, these cities are distinguished, not by *technē*, but by love. "Two loves created two cities", he famously wrote: "The love of God to the point of contempt of self" is the City of God, while the "love of self to the point of contempt of God" is the City of Man.[6] Even nowadays, this distinction runs through all of human life. We can flee our modern cities, but we can never flee the problem of the self. It is love of God alone that creates the true city, but one that is ours only in the next life. This conviction is the resistance movement of the Christian in a technological age—and it is in mountain wilderness that we can go to recover it.

The break day was at last dragging to an end when the new recruits arrived. Eight fresh-faced, eager young guys would join us on the trail for our three-day trek toward Leadville. Despite the fact that they were over-packed and under-trained, we were edified by their enthusiasm and generally optimistic. But all that was about to change.

Rain continued to fall as our preparations concluded. Tomorrow looked soggy and the terrain, formidable. Regardless, we were desperate to shake off the restlessness of the rest day and return to the trail. We had felt the enticements of modern comforts, the siren songs of our technological world. But together we set our resolve again toward the backcountry. And as the twelve of us lay down to sleep in that one-bedroom condo, I heard Casey turn to Luke and, albeit without affection, say "good night".

Perhaps this would all work out in the end.

---

[6] Augustine, *The City of God*, XIV.28.

10

THE BOND OF THE UNIVERSE

Walking is a series of imbalances. Every step forward destabilizes the self. With points of contact removed, we are rendered vulnerable, at risk to fall. Such is the simple act of taking a step—the most natural thing in the world.

That morning, I realized that the groups joining us on the Colorado Trail were themselves a series of imbalances. But with this new group, I sensed hesitancy. During our first days on the trail, the Fellowship had struggled, but always gave the sense that they knew the risks and could endure the hardships. But now things felt different.

Our principal task of the day was to gain Searle and Kokomo Passes, which, at present, were some 3,000 feet above us. It was to be an extended passage above treeline, which would make us hustle; if we weren't moving fast enough, we would likely encounter the usual afternoon thunderstorm. The morning had the residual clouds of yesterday's storm, which stood as a warning for what was to come.

The day began in a jovial manner. The wooded air was fresh and penetrating, drenched from the day before. Our bodies felt strong and invigorated by the day of rest; and the new recruits stepped onto the trail with youthful enthusiasm. Always at the front, I became accustomed to the silence of Cody and Casey, a hallmark of their morning routine. Behind them, I could hear the clamor of the group in conversation, their tone manifesting something likened to an optimistic oblivion of what the day would bring. As this new group was composed largely of engineering students, their content was strictly academic. As we twisted and turned upon wooded switchbacks, I could hear fragments of conversations about nuclear fusion and fission and whatever else occupies the minds of engineers. After this, they became known as "the Symposium". With their heads in the clouds, one wondered if they were aware of their feet.

At last we turned northward, and the grade leveled off. Reaching the meadow that we would follow to treeline, we saw him—our first moose. To say that I am skittish around moose is an understatement. But as Luke and Cody noted, this one had picked up our scent long before we saw him and made his way to the far side of the meadow. Unlike the unruly moose attempting to be an altar boy at my last encounter, this one was quietly enjoying the creek-side serenity of the damp morning. Apparently, the primary intention of moose was not just to kill humans. He watched us, and we him, and all was quiet on that meadowed front. At last, we hit treeline and saw the path to the pass.

The serenity of the moose sighting had impressed upon me the fact that the universe was actually quite intelligible. Everything was acting according to its being. Trees were being trees, moose were "moosing" around. Creation felt symphonic. Everything from the wildflowers below to the stratus clouds above spoke of order and design. The ancients had a word for this—one that would in time become intensely meaningful for Christians. They called it *logos*.

Some words are impossible to translate—and *logos* is to be counted among them. Polyvalent in its essence, *logos* can be defined as "word, speech, discourse, thought, reason, and meaning". Rooted in the verb *legein* ("to gather, bind, link, or unite"), *logos* was employed by the Greeks to describe the unifying link of all creation. First described by Heraclitus around 500 b.c., *logos* was more than a principle of unity; it was the idea upon which the wise man lived. Plato would develop this intuition of *logos* as the mind, distinguishing it as the agent of creation that he called the *demiurge*. Stoic philosophers such as Cleante and Seneca saw in it the harmony of the universe, governed by the divine spirit. And at the end of the pre-Christian era, the great Jewish philosopher Philo would see the *logos* as the first power emanating from God, calling it "the bond of the universe".

For the Christian, this philosophical history is significant because it elucidates the truly incredible opening line of the Gospel of Saint John: "In the beginning was the Word (*logos*), and the Word was with God, and the Word was God" (Jn 1:1). This fundamental description of the God-man, Jesus Christ, as *logos*, is quite possibly the most revolutionary idea in the history of human thought. With the coming of the Second Person of the Trinity in the event of the Incarnation, the bond of the universe is revealed; not as a mystical force or impersonal spirit, but as God himself made man. Christianity is the transformative synthesis of Jewish history and Greek thought, the two great rivers of the meaningfulness of reality that came to a confluence in the Roman world of Jesus. And to designate him, a man, as *logos* became the most foundational claim that the world was established upon. Jesus is now the key to interpreting reality; for just as he was "in the beginning with God", so too "all things were made through him, and without him was not anything made that was made" (Jn 1:2–3).

Jesus, the *logos* or "reason" of God, was the fulfillment of Greek metaphysical speculation. This means that to enter into his life, which we call theological faith, is entirely reasonable. Faith and reason belong together and only make sense in light of each other. As John Paul II wrote: "Faith and reason are like two wings on which the human spirit rises to the contemplation of truth; and God has placed in the human heart a desire to know the truth—in a word, to know himself—so that, by knowing and loving God, men and women may also come to the fullness of truth about themselves."[1] Faith and reason are nuptially wedded in the revelation of Jesus Christ, the *logos*. Standing in creation, we come to see the intelligibility of all things according to this new, unified form. Things in themselves are meaningful because God is himself the fullness of meaning. It is this seminal conviction that guides this vision of reality, the key without which the Christian cannot understand himself or the world of things.

But what of a world that is now post-Christian? When faith in Christ goes, so too does reason. This began in a significant way when Descartes reduced the universe to human thought. Reason, no longer the bond of the universe and the meaningfulness of all things, was imprisoned in the human mind. The subsequent attempt to rationalize reality was an imposition on things, not a disclosure from the *logos*. In the centuries that followed, this latent Cartesian skepticism not only eclipsed faith and demurred reason; it set the stage for the age of nihilism.

I was reminded of this fundamental choice between *logos* and nihilism on a climb in the Elk Range, a western neighbor to our present location on Searle Pass. We were ascending Snowmass Peak from the southwest, on a long, extended class 3 scramble known as the "S" ridge. Arriving at the summit, we found there quite possibly the most perfect, naturally constructed altar ever created on a mountaintop. As I began to set up for Mass, I saw

---

[1] Pope John Paul II, Encyclical Letter *Fides et Ratio* (September 14, 1998), no. 1.

two other climbers had just arrived at the summit. In an effort to normalize the fact that, once again, I looked like some crazy druid in strangely vested garb, I turned to them and said: "I'm a Catholic priest, and we are about to say Mass—you are welcome to join us." Without missing a beat, one of the two responded: "Thanks. We are going to be over here smoking weed—you are welcome to join us." We naturally departed on awkward yet agreed upon terms. But it was after Mass that I noticed the deeper significance of this strange situation. Reading the register of climbers on the summit of the peak, both parties had noted the last name inscribed in the book. Two days prior, the last man to stand on the summit began his descent and fell to his death. We all felt an existential eeriness in the air and responded in our own way: the escape from self in the experience of psychotropics or the turn toward God in the Eucharistic offering of the Mass.

It is easy to speak of the coherence of reality when we gaze upon the natural beauty of mountaintops. But it is in the face of suffering and death that the question of *logos* becomes difficult, and the logic of nihilism, a temptation. Without the culmination of *logos* in the death and Resurrection of Jesus Christ, the question of a meaningful human reality does in fact break down, and ultimately terminate, in the seeming conquest of meaninglessness. In the *logos*, von Balthasar affirms, the Christian "fights his way through the meaninglessness of the world ... meaning's revolt against the meaninglessness of dying."[2]

But we discover the true significance of *logos* when we realize what it points to. "Reason's summit", Giussani writes, "is the perception of the existence of the mystery."[3]

---

[2] H. U. von Balthasar, *You Crown the Year with Your Goodness: Radio Sermons*, trans. Graham Harrison (San Francisco: Ignatius Press, 1989), 97.

[3] L. Giussani, *At the Origin of the Christian Claim*, trans. Viviane Hewitt (Montreal: McGill-Queen's University Press, 1998), 6.

Together at the summit of Snowmass, we few humans saw that we were likewise at the summit of reason—a height not high enough to comprehend the inestimable conundrum of death. For the Christian, reason opens into mystery—for it is mystery, and not reason, that is the final word and, ultimately, the true measure of all things. If we settle for anything less, we precondition our thought, confining it to something inhuman, and are led to the threshold of nihilistic despair. Reason is not the measure of reality; the mystery, which we call God, is the measure. And only according to his self-disclosure in Christian revelation does the ellipsis of human life close together in that mysterious word *logos*. As Ratzinger concludes:

> The concept of *logos* has been at the very center of our Christian faith in God. *Logos* signifies reason, meaning, or even "word"—a meaning, therefore, that is Word, that is relationship, that is creative. The God who is *logos* guarantees the intelligibility of the world, the intelligibility of our existence.... The world comes from reason, and this reason is a Person, is Love.[4]

What we first found remarkable we now find incredible—that the *logos* is the God-man as well as the center of divine love. In God, the meaningfulness of creation is enveloped into the mystery of Trinitarian love. And this is the true bond of the universe.

As we approached Searle Pass, the Symposium was growing quietly mutinous. Having reached our high point just above 12,000 feet, the clouds threatened a storm,

[4] J. Ratzinger, *Introduction to Christianity*, trans. J. R. Foster (San Francisco: Ignatius Press, 2004), 26.

but nothing more. We had a two-mile lateral jaunt to Kokomo Pass before beginning our huge descent to the Cataract Creek basin—and safety below the treeline. But the Symposium was frantic about the storm and wanted to turn back. At this point, returning to Copper was just as perilous. I had seen these clouds before and believed we could make it. It was decided—and we set out on another series of imbalances.

By the time we reached Kokomo, the sun had reached its climax, filling the now cloudless skies with its radiant warmth. We had arrived at what was an epicenter of Rocky Mountain glory: to the north was the Gore Range, peaks like sheaved blades ready for war; to the east stood the harrowing passages of the Tenmile-Mosquito Range, giants we had traversed two days before; and to the west, most glorious of all, we beheld the Mount of the Holy Cross—Colorado's greatest legacy of mystery. As early as the mid-1800s, when Americans looked upon this Thomas Moran's painting of the Mount, with its carved couloir-shaped cross, they saw in it a sign of the destiny that awaited our nation on this continent. For our band of fledging brothers, it was a sign of the hope of Christ in the Cross. Now leaving the heights of Kokomo, we descended again to the wooden maze, making our way to our next great challenge—the wilderness expanse of the Mount of the Holy Cross.

11

THE DWARF AND
THE TRAGEDIAN

Descending the basin of Cataract Creek, the day's seventeen-mile march would lead us first over Tennessee Pass and then southward into the Holy Cross Wilderness. This would begin a long set of days passing along the eastern side of the Sawatch Mountains—the largest range that we would encounter (apart from the San Juans at the end of the trail). Having spent a number of years climbing the Sawatch peaks, I knew them to be giants.

Prior to ascending Tennessee Pass, we had to traverse a long narrow valley that gave a strange impression. Indeed, it felt haunted—not by ghosts, but by the spirit of history. Just eighty years ago, this valley was the site of Camp Hale, the famous training center of the Tenth Mountain Division. At its peak in the early 1940s, the place was home to fifteen thousand soldiers. Being attached to the Fifth Army Infantry, it was comprised of men preparing for mountain warfare. Inspired by the mountain tactics of the Finnish Army against invading Russians, these soldiers spent their years at Camp Hale training in various forms of mountaineering and skiing. Though the original intention of the Tenth Mountain Division was to assuage a Nazi land assault from Canada, the soldiers were to be sent to the Italian front of the Second World War. Their fame was won in the Apennine Mountains, a range that runs spine-like, north-south, through Italy. The German Army held what was called "the winter line", which being an unassailable position just north of Florence, impeded the Allied Forces from breaking into the Po River Valley and liberating the north of Italy. In February of 1945, the Tenth Mountain Division broke the line through a strategic attack on the Riva Ridge and Mount Belvedere. The Germans were caught completely off guard as a thousand soldiers rock climbed a flanking face and seized their fortifications. The heroism of the Tenth broke the line and routed the Germans all the way back to the Alps before their final surrender in May of that year. But it came at a cost—by the end of the Italian invasion, the causalities of the Tenth Mountain Division had reached a significant 25 percent.[1]

As we passed through that valley, the only visible sign of this remarkable history was a placard near the road. But we had other things on our mind; we were on the brink of our first trail casualty. The last few miles up the pass, a member of the Symposium lagged behind, and when we broke for lunch, I pulled him aside. "If you want this," I offered, "we can get you through it—but I need to know you want it." I was shocked when he responded, "I quit."

This was a turning point on the trail, one that unsettled me for days. For many years, I had prided myself on being able to get anyone through any challenge in the mountains. I didn't realize my tacit expectation that every guy who stepped on the trail would finish with us. That was no longer the case, and there was nothing we could do about it. He hitchhiked to town and, from there, back to city life.

---

[1] Cf. Peter Shelton, *Climb to Conquer: The Untold Story of World War II's 10th Mountain Division* (New York: Scribner, 2011).

Five minutes later, the heavens opened, and we got hammered by hail. I guess if he didn't want it, he left at the right time.

Passing through the memory of that war training camp recalled to us the reality of history. Life in the backcountry can give the impression that history doesn't matter, that it has no bearing on the simplicity of our natural surroundings. But man, who belongs to creation, also belongs to history. As moderns, we struggle to embrace history, because we find in it the presence of evil. We grew up studying all the things "bad people do", sometimes reduced to the "bad structures" others have created. But the Christian is not satisfied with relegating evil to external circumstances. The problem is inside us. As the prophet Jeremiah lamented: "The heart is deceitful above all things, and desperately corrupt; who can understand it?" (Jer 17:9). Evil resides in moral form in the human heart, and this we call sin. And sin, in its essence, is self-deception—a human problem that requires an answer.

This truth is powerfully depicted in C. S. Lewis' *The Great Divorce*. It begins at a bus stop in Hell, where souls load up and depart for a visit to Heaven. Upon their arrival, Lewis portrays the encounters between the visitors and residents. Their dialogues reveal to us that Hell is not so much a punishment as it is self-imposed. The visitors are invited to stay in Heaven, but only on the condition that they renounce the things keeping them in Hell. For the most part, they refuse; steeped in self-deception, they rationalize their way out of the invitation. The central point is arresting—that Hell is constituted by earthly loves, unredeemed by the love of God.

One of the most striking vignettes in the book is a conversation between a married couple named Sarah and Frank.

Sarah, now in Heaven, and Frank in Hell, are reunited during the latter's bus trip. As with the other interactions, Sarah beckons Frank to give up his self-imposed Hell and join her in Heaven. But Frank is depicted in a very strange manner, as "a dwarf and a tragedian". What we learn of Frank is that he is so consumed by jealousy and resentment that his personality is literally bifurcated. This reveals the fragmentary nature of sin as well as the way in which it enslaves us. The small dwarf is holding the large tragedian captive by a chain around his neck. In time, Sarah is able to free the tragedian from the dwarf, bringing Frank back to life. Her main lesson is this: "What we called love down there was mostly the craving to be loved. In the main, I loved you for my own sake: because I needed you."[2] Even for Sarah, earthly loves were incomplete until they were enveloped in the love of God. Frank became a dwarf and tragedian, not because he lacked love, but because his love was not authenticated by divine love. And this is why sin is self-deception.

Sin, Aquinas tells us, is two things in one: a turning from God (*superbia*) and a turning toward a passing good (*cupiditas*).[3] The combination of these lead to a promethean attempt to become God through the creation of an idol, a projection of self-idolatry. Because this occurred in our first parents, Adam and Eve, human nature is fallen and mortally wounded. It remains good but damaged, in need of healing. Second to the doctrine of creation, the doctrine of original sin is essential for understanding the *raison d'être* of the whole Christian life. "It is almost (or entirely) impossible to avoid the illusion that man knows from himself what love is, and how it is to be practiced."[4] This sober insight from

---

[2] C. S. Lewis, *The Great Divorce* (New York: HarperOne, 2001), 125.
[3] Cf. J. Pieper, *The Concept of Sin* (South Bend: St. Augustine's Press, 2001).
[4] H. U. von Balthasar, "Vocation", in *Communio* 37 (Spring 2010): 125.

von Balthasar expresses why running into the backcountry doesn't get us away from sin. The problem is our illusory loves, those that make us dwarfs and tragedians.

In my years on the high peaks, I have had too many dangerous experiences, arising out of the self-deception of my sin. An example that comes to mind is on Castle Peak, a relatively harmless mountain situated on the east side of the Elk Range. I had heard about a geothermal hot spring called Conundrum on the far side and decided that instead of just climbing the mountain, we would backpack over it to enjoy the springs. But the descent ended up being a perilous minefield of falling talus. Though we arrived at the springs after many hours of bushwacking, my friend was afflicted with pulmonary edema. Instead of enjoying the springs, he laid there gasping for air as his lungs filled with fluid—and we were above 11,000 feet, twenty miles from the nearest town.

He made it out alright, but the lesson was learned; living in self-deception is sinful and can cause great harm to others. If we continue to reject the reality of sin in ourselves, we will never come to know the truth of love. And if we never know the truth of love, we will fall victim to the belief that life is constituted by the will to power. This is the human story—the drama of good and evil, the story of the will to power or the will to love. As a Roman soldier once inscribed on a stone in North Africa: "I, the Captain of a Legion of Rome, serving in the desert of Libya, have learnt and pondered this truth: 'there are in life but two things, Love and Power, and no one has both.'"[5]

In the life and person of Jesus Christ, this dialectic of love and power reaches its apex. The inner, hidden logic

[5] M. Muggeridge, *The Infernal Grove: Chronicles of Wasted Time: Number 2* (New York: HarperCollins, 1974), 67.

of power, so often guised as love, is drawn fully into the light. On the Cross, Christ reveals the depth of power-lessness that belongs alone to divine love, the source of all things. In Jesus we see the definitive conquest of power-less love over the world's love of power. To assent to this victory is to assume the name of Christian and begin the laborious undertaking of *metanoia*, i.e., converting one's mind and heart to the love of God. As Saint Paul describes: "Have this mind among yourselves, which was in Christ Jesus, who, though he was in the form of God, did not count equality with God a thing to be grasped, but emp-tied himself, taking the form of a servant, being born in the likeness of men" (Phil 2:5–7). Taking on the mind of Christ is the way to freedom from sin. Contrary to the false methods of casuistry or muscular Christianity, con-version from sin toward God is the restoration of loves that Christ alone can accomplish in us. And that is the source of our most immense freedom.

By evening, we had arrived at our alpine campsite. Bur-ied deep within the Holy Cross Wilderness, we tucked into the side of Moser Lake. As Mass began, the quiet amphitheater of rocks below the face of Galena Moun-tain were held captive. The Symposium was worn out and understandably nervous, as one of their own no longer shared the communion of the trail. As the sun set beyond the neighboring Homestake Peak, the day closed with the sudden brilliance of those last gasps of illuminating beauty. Night fell. All was still, and the world was at peace—until the attack of the mosquitos began.

I guess we do indeed live in a fallen world, and perfec-tion will have to wait for the next.

12

ISLANDS OF HUMANITY

Galena Peak was catching fire as the breaking dawn illumined the west. Breakfast at our camp on Moser Lake was not hasty, but certainly in motion, as the day before us would be challenging. We were now turning decidedly south, leaving behind the last of the Holy Cross Wilderness. It was to be our last day with the men of the Symposium, and our task was clear—to get them to the trail exit point where we would make for our resupply in the town of Leadville.

Today would be long and arduous—nineteen miles and 3,500 feet of elevation gain. Warming up on a series of sustained rolling foothills, we would have an extended climb to a pass above Bear Lake, followed by a massive descent and circumnavigation of the vast and impressive Turquoise Lake. From there it was another steady series of rollers until at last we reached our resupply at the trailhead of Mount Massive. Massive, the peak under which most of the day would be spent, now appeared as quite the understatement.

After several hours, we stopped for an early Mass and lunch at a quiet and hidden stream. The sun was already oppressive, and the cool shade felt restorative. This would be the most difficult moment for the Symposium—calling forth from a new level of mental endurance to push their bodies above and beyond the pass.

As was customary, Casey wandered off just as we were again setting out on the trail. What he would do on these nature walks (or what he would kill) was beyond me. But we had a symposium of anxious engineers to get to Turquoise Lake, and he was not my immediate concern. Our pace was steady but slow, and after an hour, I realized Casey was still not with us. Another hour passed, and no sign of Casey. By now, approaching the top of the pass and not seeing him, we began to get worried. I mentally replayed my last words of instruction to Casey: "Make sure you cross the stream and take the trail to the south." If he didn't cross the stream, he would head on the wrong trail due eastward. Now at the top of the pass, we knew he didn't turn south.

Galena Peak at sunrise recalled a clear memory from my days in the Alps. I was with several students climbing up and around the Klein Matterhorn, a small peak nestled between the Breithorn and the Matterhorn high above Zermatt. At the summit, I saw a beautifully wood-carved crucifix. Below the body of our Lord were written the words "*mehr mensch sein*" (be more human). This struck me at once as one of the most powerful and important insights into the essence of Christianity that I had ever seen.

The Roman rhetor Marius Victorinus described his conversion to the Christian faith in these words: "When I met Christ, I discovered myself to be a man."[1] Far from being a religion that transcends and eclipses humanity, coming to know the person of Jesus Christ is the source

[1] L. Giussani, *To Give One's Life for the Work of Another* (Montreal: McGill-Queen's University Press, 2022), 51. Cf. L. Giussani, S. Alberto, and J. Prades, *Generating Traces in the History of the World: New Traces in the Christian Experience*, trans. Patrick Stevenson (Montreal: McGill-Queen's University Press, 2010), 9.

of the realization of humanity. If the Incarnation is the key to understanding God's method for revealing himself, then it is precisely in humanity that divinity is encountered. This is why a Swiss climber had the intuition to write under a crucifix "*mehr mensch sein*". The God-man on that Cross is the source of true humanity; for he himself is the totally and fully human man. To know him in the encounter of faith is to discover the truth of one's own humanity. Being human is then not something to be surpassed or eliminated—it is the condition of everything.

The *Catechism* teaches that man is the "summit" of the Creator's work.[2] He alone was created for his own sake, with the capacity for relationship, knowledge, and love of God. For this reason, we can even affirm that God created everything *for* man, a gift of love entrusted to his care. What grounds us in this reality is the fact of the Incarnation. When God became man, he reestablished creation as a place of encounter. Everything is centered on this mystery: "And the Word became flesh and dwelt among us, full of grace and truth" (Jn 1:14). Only in the Incarnation is the dignity of human creatureliness understood and, thus, drawn to its supernatural fulfillment.

But the modern world is founded on a rejection of this event. In this way, it is distinctively anti–incarnational. The logic of Christ is no longer the mode for interpreting human experience, which severs any notion of salvation in him. What has supplanted it is the age-old alternative, known as Gnosticism. Rooted in the Greek word for "knowledge" (*gnosis*), Gnosticism proposes that the salvation of man occurs through a kind of spiritual knowledge. As it was the principal enemy of early Christianity, it remains forever the perennial one. What is interesting is

---

[2] *Catechism of the Catholic Church*, no. 343.

to note with the political philosopher Augusto del Noce, "that we live in a time when the new gnosis is decomposing."[3] And all this informs our secular approach to Jesus— thinking of him, not as fully man, but as a distillation of illuminating knowledge.

If humanity is the criteria to understanding the truth of Christianity, then the daily task of the Christian is to become more human. But how is this possible in a culture dominated by a gnosticizing and technological *zeitgeist?* To this question Hans Urs von Balthasar once formulated an intriguing and penetrating response:

> But what can be done amid this want of culture wrought by the machine? I suppose one can try to build islands of humanity, and in this project Christians could and should be leading; such actions may have a contagious effect on others and stimulate an asceticism which renounces the excessive goods of consumerism, simply to become more human.... From islands like this, true culture, Christian culture, may spread across the earth. Many people are athirst for it.[4]

When Christians take up the project of "becoming more human", they must begin by creating islands of humanity. We cannot survive in the oceans of nihilism, tempted by gnostic allurements, apart from these concretely lived places of Christian humanism. To be Christian means to be human because God became human. Human nature is the place where supernatural grace resides, elevating it and not eliminating it. The encounter with God does not happen in

---

[3] A. del Noce, *The Crisis of Modernity*, trans. Carlo Lancellotti (Montreal: McGill-Queen's University Press, 2015), 25.

[4] H. U. von Balthasar, *Test Everything: Hold Fast to What Is Good*, trans. Maria Shrady (San Francisco: Ignatius Press, 2012), 50–51.

some a-personal mystical sphere. The entire meeting place between God and man is in the humanity of Jesus Christ; and this changes everything. To know him is to know God; and to know him is to know humanity. Like Victorinus, we discover ourselves as human when we encounter Jesus Christ. This remains the central project of Christian existence, never more urgent than in our present day.

As a newly ordained priest, I was missioned as a college chaplain to the University of Colorado. I realized quickly the modicum of interest in attending Mass and participating in the life of the Church. But the students were restless and wanted to be more human—and that became the touchpoint. All that was needed was to create islands of humanity where this desire could experience its fulfillment in Jesus.

I discovered a series of mountain huts, built in memory of the Tenth Mountain Division in the region between Vail and Aspen (the area in which we were now passing). These huts, far more primitive than their European ancestors, were remote and rugged, situated high up in the backcountry. With no running water and electricity, they were the perfect locales to found islands of humanity. For the last thirteen years, I have taken young people to the huts, to rediscover ourselves in the human encounter with Christ. It was here that I would read quite possibly the most beautiful poetic tribute to the Incarnation, "As Kingfishers Catch Fire" by Gerard Manley Hopkins.

> As kingfishers catch fire, dragonflies draw flame;
> As tumbled over rim in roundy wells
> Stones ring; like each tucked string tells, each hung bell's
> Bow swung finds tongue to fling out broad its name;
> Each mortal thing does one thing and the same:
> Deals out that being indoors each one dwells;

Selves—goes itself; *myself* it speaks and spells,
Crying *What I do is me: for that I came.*

I say more: the just man justices;
Keeps grace: that keeps all his goings graces;
Acts in God's eye what in God's eye he is—
Chríst—for Christ plays in ten thousand places,
Lovely in limbs, and lovely in eyes not his
To the Father through the features of men's faces.

Leaving the exhausted Symposium, Luke, Cody, and I made haste back down the pass in search of Casey. And there he was, about thirty minutes behind us, charging up the mountain. As expected, he did not cross the stream and put a number of miles down toward Leadville before finally realizing that he was headed in the entirely wrong direction. The added miles for Casey would put him well over twenty-five that day; but as always, he looked unfazed.

Descending from the pass, we arrived at Timberline Creek, a tributary of Turquoise Lake and, farther down, the Arkansas River. It was moving fast and wild—and to my utter dismay, did not have a bridge or any obvious place to cross. With the entire group looking to my lead, I stepped out into the stream, fatefully mis-stepped, and made a full send into the water. Pack and poles flying, my body was suddenly being swept away by the voraciously impending waterflow. At last I regained my footing, recollected most of my gear, and dragged myself from the creek. I was completely soaked, and we still had six miles to go. Getting my bearings, I looked up and saw something a quarter mile upstream. It was a bridge, and standing up on it, dry and victorious, was Casey waving with an air of condescension. "Bastard," I thought, "now you remember to cross the stream."

13

A KNIFE'S EDGE

Every climber who sets out to summit Colorado's fifty-four high peaks knows that at some point, he will face a ridge that inspires awe and engenders fear—the Knife Edge. Tucked into the center of the harrowing range of the Elk Mountains lies its home on Capitol Peak. Considered by many to be the state's most challenging fourteener, passage over the Knife Edge is required to gain the summit. Approaching the ridge from the north, you work your way first to a small peak known as "K2" before stepping onto the 200-foot stretch of granite. Stepping onto the Knife Edge, you find yourself standing on a mere six-inch walkway. The experience is one of immediate vertigo; down to the right and left are vertical drops of several thousand feet. No ledges, no barriers—just the pure expansiveness of verticality that defies measure.

The Knife Edge is an image of how intensely vulnerable the mountains can make us feel. It is a reason, I believe, that we are drawn to them. But this defies our modern sensibility for safety and control. Nevertheless, we long for wild and vulnerable places; because without them, something in us dies.

Unlike the Knife Edge, the Colorado Trail does not traverse daring cliffs and engender vulnerability. For this reason, I thought we would be safe, with only mitigated risks.

But that all changed on day thirteen, when we picked up our third new group on the trail. Setting out across the base of Mount Elbert, we would soon experience a vulnerability far greater than any Knife Edge.

♦ ♦ ♦

From the Latin word *vulnus*, meaning "wound", vulnerability can be most basically defined as "wound-ability". It is a quality of being exposed, of risk and uncertainty. The basic human response to this state is dread and avoidance at all costs. We are made for safety, which is why it is natural to remove occasions of vulnerability.

But moving more deeply into the mystery of life, we see that vulnerability is something more, something that can't actually be avoided. The human heart is, by its very nature, vulnerable; and no matter what we attempt to do, we cannot rid ourselves of it. As C. S. Lewis aptly notes:

> To love at all is to be vulnerable. Love anything, and your heart will certainly be wrung and possibly be broken. If you want to make sure of keeping it intact, you must give your heart to no one, not even to an animal. Wrap it carefully round with hobbies and little luxuries; avoid all entanglements; lock it up safe in the casket or coffin of your selfishness. But in that casket—safe, dark, motionless, airless—it will change. It will not be broken; it will become unbreakable, impenetrable, irredeemable.[1]

The nature of love requires vulnerability of heart. In the language of Scripture, this is "the heart of flesh" in contrast to the "heart of stone" (cf. Ezek 11:14–21). Living things are vulnerable; dead things are invulnerable. Such

---

[1] C. S. Lewis, *The Four Loves* (New York: Harcourt Brace, 1991), 121.

is the nature of life that it can be wounded. One must decide: Will I risk being wounded in order to gain the possibility of communion? If I choose to love, I will no doubt become "out of control". But this is part of the path to human perfection. Love changes us, and as John Henry Newman wrote, "to live is to change, and to be perfect is to have changed often."[2] Hearts of stone do not change; but vulnerable hearts of flesh, capable of change, can become perfect in love.

The poet Rilke once described life as being "on the cliffs of the human heart".[3] When we deny this "cliff-like" nature of human existence, we become *mediocre*. From the Greek words *medio* (halfway) and *ikros* (peak), the mediocre man is the one who stops halfway up the peak. This is typically done because of a refusal for more risk. But as von Hildebrand writes: "If we want to avoid risk, we should have to stop living, for to live is to take risks."[4] The mediocre heart is one that sets out to love and then, when feeling the exposure, freezes in a desperate attempt at self-preservation. But this act is as deadly to human love as it is to stop halfway on the Knife Edge.

Vulnerability is not just essential to love; it is a requirement for knowledge of truth and relationship with God. So much of the latent practical atheism that dominates our modern world is connected to the loss of a lived and felt vulnerability to the reality of things as they are. But in order to open oneself to the reality of God, we must divest ourselves of the project of ego protection. "Truth",

[2] J. H. Newman, *Essay on the Development of Doctrine* (South Bend: University of Notre Dame Press, 1989), 40.

[3] R. M. Rilke, "Exposed on the Cliffs of the Heart", in *The Selected Poetry of Rainer Maria Rilke*, trans. Stephen Mitchell (New York: Vintage International, 1989), 143.

[4] D. von Hildebrand, *The Heart* (South Bend: St. Augustine's Press, 2007), 37.

Ratzinger maintains, "is always perilous. But only in the measure in which man risks the passion of truth does he become a man."[5] What is at stake if we don't risk embracing the truth? Our very humanity. The human intellect, far surpassing the sensate abilities of animals, must open itself to the truth and render the heart vulnerable for its reception. What undergirds this risk? The experience that the grounds of reality are the powerlessness of love. And this love is either God or it is not love at all. As von Balthasar observes: "He encounters his limitations, feels his powerlessness, senses a boundless disillusionment with regard to himself and his life; one dear person has abandoned him, in death, another has deserted him, unfaithful; an icy wind blows through the empty place; it is time to make up his mind—God or nothingness."[6] Vulnerability belongs not just to the order of life and love, but to the reality of truth and God. And every human life experiences these moments of total exposure, which render the heart existentially vertiginous. It is impossible to pass through life without moments where one finds oneself on the knife's edge.

The most intense experiences of vulnerability happen, not on mountain cliffs, but in the drama of interpersonal relationship. We feel most vulnerable in the presence of others. Our choice is whether to embrace this and allow it to be transfigured into self-giving love. Vulnerability means to disclose one's poverty in such a way as it can be encountered. If it is met by a true reverence, then the risk of vulnerability is catalyzed into a new, more profound experience of communion. Our fear of vulnerability is our

---

[5] J. Ratzinger, *Principles of Catholic Theology: Building Stones for a Fundamental Theology*, trans. Mary Frances McCarthy (San Francisco: Ignatius Press, 1989), 33.

[6] H. U. von Balthasar, *Who Is a Christian?*, trans. Frank Davidson (San Francisco: Ignatius Press, 2014), 107.

inability to love, first, our own poverty and, then, subsequently, the poverty we see in others. As Guardini soberly observes: "Human relationships are so muddled that we all seem to be living in spite of rather than with our fellows. Human friendships are hardly ever a complete success. Love is hardly ever perfectly fulfilled."[7]

What, then, is the conclusion? What, then, is the way? Our culture is increasingly obsessed with a "victim mentality", which is nothing more than the resentment of an unredeemed vulnerability. For the Christian, the answer is forgiveness. It alone draws vulnerability into the tender embrace of divine love. Forgiveness, the "giving forth" of one's judgment and assessment of things, is the place where fear terminates and the heart reopens and again becomes flesh. "Forgiveness establishes communion", wrote Ratzinger.[8] Not therapy, not spirituality—not even vulnerability in itself—but forgiveness alone is what fulfills the desires of the heart. It is here that one must speak of the event of Jesus Christ, whose death was an atoning sacrifice for the forgiveness of sins. What is so remarkable about the Christian claim is that in God becoming man, he renders himself vulnerable. Without this, there is no forgiveness of sins, no redemption of man. "By his wounds you have been healed" (1 Pet 2:24).

Today was supposed to be simple and straightforward—twelve miles and 1,200 feet around the east side of Mount Elbert and down to the far side of the Twin Lakes. But

[7] R. Guardini, *The Living God*, trans. Stanley Godman (New York: Pantheon, 1957), 67.

[8] J. Ratzinger, *Introduction to Christianity*, trans. J. R. Foster (San Francisco: Ignatius Press, 2004), 336.

within the first few hours, the group fell into diaspora, scattered across the mountainside. Eventually, we recollected at five miles in and assessed the situation. Luke's job was to sweep that day, to take the back of the line and make sure that the group held together from the back. But I hadn't seen him that day, and I was getting concerned. We knew why he was gone—my priest friend was struggling immensely, and Luke was by his side. Like all the groups who would join us on the trail, they were a mix: men who were trained up, had the right gear, and were mentally prepared for the challenge, and then the others, who for whatever reason were not ready to, and perhaps not capable of, making the trip. We had lost our first guy on the prior section; now it seemed as if we might lose a whole group.

At this point I made another difficult decision. I had to turn my priest friend back, only five miles into a four-day journey. He was going back to the car, his hike was over—and I had to ask Cody and Casey to make a sacrifice to make it happen. They were to drop their packs, run back five miles to Luke, get the priest to the car, and then return to camp. This would double the mileage and elevation for the day and require a physical feat.

I continued on with the remnant. Passing Mount Elbert, we looked down upon the valley of the Twin Lakes, where the sun glittered and danced upon the waters. Our camp was on the far side and still many miles ahead. But once we descended from the mountain, we would have to pass through what looked like the Mojave Desert. And it was here that the wheels started to fall off. The men were faltering—and this was supposed to be the easy day. After many hours of drudgery, we finally arrived at camp, vulnerable and raw. And I was deeply concerned over the state of things.

Our campground by the Twin Lakes was not far from Highway 82, which allowed my priest friend to drive his car around and meet us for camp that evening. He was of course humiliated by his physical performance and shamed by my decision to end his trip. The remaining group was downtrodden and battered. Cody, Casey, and Luke were tacitly indignant over my decision to invite ill-equipped men to join us. The whole enterprise seemed compromised by my decisions.

That moment was a knife's edge, the most vulnerable on the trail. For relational vulnerability is far more intense and perilous than any mountain climb. I learned that day that to be vulnerable as a leader sometime requires being wounded by your own decisions. It also means making decisions that you know will wound those who are vulnerable.

I knew what tomorrow would bring. Upon leaving camp in the morning, we would have no access out of the wilderness until we arrived at our next resupply in three days. Tomorrow's elevation gain was an astounding 4,200 feet—four times that which we had done today. Our plan had to change. Half the group would not be departing with us in the morning. Some chose this on their own, others I had to ask to leave. It felt divisive and wrong, but I knew it was our only hope.

I went to bed that night with a wounded heart.

14

THE WISDOM OF ZOSIMA

It happened that the members of the "half-group" that set out that morning were mostly in high school. This was the youngest crew that had joined us on the trail and by far the most bizarre. After a number of attempts to "culturally connect", we realized that these creatures were from a different epoch than we four grizzled thru-hikers were. When Luke asked, for example, their favorite movie of all time, they unanimously answered "Kung Fu Panda". I had not only not seen the movie—I had never even heard of it. So naturally, this became their group name.

Despite an initial push of hard work and the appearance of confidence, the Pandas were shaken by last night's conversation. They wondered if they were next to get kicked off the trail. Moreover, they sensed what was coming after lunch—a climb of impending doom known as the "man-maker". The trail would either make these pandas into men or it would send them packing for Denver.

On the southern edge of the Twin Lakes, the Colorado Trail splits: one part following the Collegiate Range on the east side, one to the west. Though the west route is far more scenic, it is also far more difficult. Given the state of our crew, we opted to hold the east route, knowing full well that it would still be a serious physical feat. In the next seventeen miles, we were to climb up out of the valley and once again gain the ridgeline of the Sawatch Range. Then descending west of Clear Creek Reservoir, the real challenge would begin—"the man-maker"—our longest sustained climb of the trail, putting the total elevation of the day well over 4,000 feet.

In 1841, Ralph Waldo Emerson wrote an essay entitled "Self-Reliance". It remains one of the most paradigmatic American philosophical reflections ever written, one which still informs how we think about society and the backcountry. Expressing the heart of his transcendentalist project, Emerson calls us to leave behind all temptations to social conformity: "Whoso would be a man", he writes, "must be a nonconformist."[1] In learning to trust, not in others, but in ourselves, we heed the call to refound human existence according to our own individual voice and not the voice of others. This is the heart of self-reliance and what would become the hallmark of the self-made American. What Emerson envisioned in this individualistic shift was a radical transformation in the life of modern man. As he writes: "It is easy to see that a greater self-reliance must work a revolution in all the offices and relations of men; in their religion; in their education; in their pursuits; their modes of living; their association; in their property; in their speculative views."[2]

I was reminded of how deeply this Emersonian call to self-reliance had penetrated our backcountry *ethos* on a recent climb up Longs Peak. Just before entering the "keyhole" and heading for the crux of the climb (known

[1] R. W. Emerson, "Self-Reliance", in *Nature and Selected Essays* (New York: Penguin Books: 2003), 178.

[2] Ibid., 195.

as the "narrows"), you are greeted by a sign that reads: "A trip, slip, or fall could be fatal. Rescue is difficult and could take hours or days. Self-reliance is essential." Longs Peak, though by no means the most difficult of Colorado's fourteeners, has claimed the most lives—and for this reason, one is advised to go no farther than the Keyhole without the quality of self-reliance.

Now, granted, self-reliance is an uncontested requirement for a climber. The prudential judgment that guides the course of one's actions above treeline is no doubt essential, and the absence of this has resulted in many ill-equipped people caught in the narrows in a thunderstorm. One must have the internal physical and psychological resolve to get oneself out of any situation; and in this sense, we can speak of self-reliance in a positive sense.

But self-reliance needs a qualification, or rather a purification from its Emersonian form. As we headed toward the "man-maker", I reflected on how my self-reliance was the problem causing—and not the solution to—some of my greatest failures in the backcountry. The most stark and grave example happened on Columbia Peak, the mountain that we were currently traversing. I was a young priest in my late twenties, who prided himself on getting anyone up and down a fourteener. But that day the mountains called my bluff. Too large a group was led out at too slow a pace, and the inevitable happened—that weather that looked "fine" had in fact turned into a dark and ominous thunderstorm that was set on a perfect trajectory to meet us at the summit of the peak. The panic-stricken group took off down the long-extended shoulder of its northern face. And in a moment of desperate decision to lose elevation, I called them all off the shoulder to descend a long gully, a more direct route down to treeline. It was then that the heavens opened, and amidst the unspeakable danger of lightning and thunder, the rains turned the loose gully rock into a vertical bowling alley.

At this point, things got worse: I heard a crack and watched a massive boulder dislodge and head straight for the group below. As the boulder plunged toward a guy and a girl, in a heroic and instinctive moment, I saw the guy jump to push the girl out of the way and take the boulder straight on. Running down to him, I saw that his leg had taken the brunt of the impact and that he was unable to walk. With the majority of the group far below us, there was only one option: to carry him down the remaining 2,000 feet to safety at treeline. To my great fortune, the man was rather compact and, once on my shoulders, felt like a large koala bear. But as the rains continued to fall, the loose talus rock of the gully made our movements all the more impossible. We were both trying to compensate for my falls, which only exacerbated the problem. Finally, we both realized that the only way down would be for him to entrust himself totally to me—and no matter how I fidgeted, slipped, or even fell, he would have to resign himself completely to me. The koala bear was faithful to this call, and we got down the gully. He made it to the hospital, and everything ended up alright.

In the days that followed, I was left with the tremendous guilt of my decisions as a leader. My self-reliance (my "knowing better") was the reason we made for the summit despite the coming storm and also dropped into the gully instead of taking the safer route on the shoulder of the mountain. Self-reliance may be noble within the framework of Emerson's individualism, but the second you apply it to the life of a community, it can lead to destruction. As Saint Ignatius notes in his *Spiritual Exercises*, this mentality espouses three others—self-will, self-interest, and self-love. These, he describes, are the foremost enemies of the soul.

What, then, is the response to self-reliance? Humble love. It is this that expresses the deep human need for reliance on others, especially on God. As we noted in prior letters, by the nature of our very existence, we depend on God and are called to discover ourselves through dependence on others. Humans cannot exist without this, and it is for this reason that the Christian vision of life rejects the wholesale notion of self-reliance, seeing life as a school for reliance on others. When we free ourselves of self-reliance in the spiritual life and embrace the way of humble love, we become capable of a life of deep service and a total gift of self. It is this way of life that finds expression in no better place than in the words of Jesus Christ himself.

> And Jesus called them to him and said to them, "You know that those who are supposed to rule over the Gentiles lord it over them, and their great men exercise authority over them. But it shall not be so among you; but whoever would be great among you must be your servant, and whoever would be first among you must be slave of all. For the Son of man also came not to be served but to serve, and to give his life as a ransom for many." (Mk 10:42–45)

This Gospel imperative found a unique literary translation in the writings of Fyodor Dostoevsky, who formulated the notion of humble love as a response to the logic of self-reliant power. In conversation with the Russian *starets* Zosima, the young Alyosha Karamazov is told these beautiful words by his spiritual father: " 'Shall I take it by force or humble love?' Always resolve to take it by humble love. If you so resolve once and for all, you will be able to overcome the whole world. A loving humility is a terrible power, the most powerful of all, nothing compares with it."[3] Just as a radicalized, individual notion of self-reliance blinds us to the reality of love, it eclipses the notion of humility. A distinctively Christian virtue, humility is not some kind of self-effacing and pathetic "thinking less of ourselves". It conveys, as Saint Thomas Aquinas explains, "the notion of a praiseworthy self-abasement to the lowest place", rooted first in man's subjection to God.[4] But most importantly, the virtue of humility is illumined by the way in which God reveals his inner life, and thereby in the way he comes to live among and redeem man.

We don't often think to pair humility and love, as Dostoevsky does in the wisdom of Zosima. But in an age where love has become a weapon of ideology, all the more must it be grounded in this uniquely Christian virtue. Humility is the capacity to know the truth of things and to understand oneself in relation to them. When God, who is the fullness of reality, reveals himself and communicates his life in grace, man is able to know and love the reality of things in a new and more profound way. This means embracing limitations and desiring a healthy reliance on others. No man is an island, and it is this basic fact that directs our course of action in society and in the backcountry. Only the presence of love allows me to see something truly. As Guardini reflects: "To be authentic, genuine love must always respect the other person in his integrity, recognize in him the right to be himself, and desire that he become himself more and more. By means of this perspicacity love succeeds in seeing the other person as he truly is."[5]

---

[3] F. Dostoevsky, *The Brothers Karamazov*, trans. Richard Pevear and Larissa Volokhonsky (New York: Everyman's Library, 1992), 319.

[4] Thomas Aquinas, *Summa Theologiae*, II-II, q. 161, a. 1.

[5] R. Guardini, *The Life of Faith*, trans. John Chapin (Westminster: Newman Press, 1961), 60.

To live in the reality of God is to be conquered by humble love. Christ alone is the man who truly sees. He is free *from* self-reliance because he lives totally *for* the Father. In him we discover the ultimate, dynamic unity: the humble giftedness of love is the transformative synthesis of human life and the mystery of everything.

By midday the next major problem arose in our group. One of our company, an experienced backpacker, was having foot problems. When we removed his shoes, we saw, not human feet, but bloody stubs. These were absolutely the worst blisters anyone had experienced. He could no longer walk—and we were nowhere near an exit point. The man had to embrace the humiliation of ending his trip early, die of his self-reliance, and allow my trusted lieutenants Cody and Casey somehow to get him out of the backcountry.

As they departed, Luke and I attempted to galvanize the Kung Fu Pandas for the most challenging section of the trail. Steep switchbacks in endless repetition beat down the crew—but in the end they persevered. As with all groups, some were stronger than others; but with this group, they would finish the man-maker together and celebrate at the top their graduation from adolescence.

By the time we reached camp that evening, the rain was pouring. Tucked into the hillside along Pine Creek, we were now officially in the middle of nowhere. Cody and Casey arrived after a successful evacuation, and we had another awkward nine-man Mass in my four-man tent. Afterward, as the rains subsided, we experienced one of the most serene and Edenic evenings of the entire month. Sitting by the creek, we fished for small brook trout and smoked pipes, read T. S. Eliot, and discussed the deeper things of life. It was an event of communion, one which the prospects of self-reliance could never attain. It was a painful and arduous day, conquered by humble love. And in the words of Guardini, who had by now become our Zosima, we reflected on a most memorable night: "To those who love deeply, everything becomes an event within the sphere of their love."[6]

---

[6]R. Guardini as quoted in L. Giussani, *The Risk of Education*, trans. Rosanna M. Giammanco (New York: Crossroad, 2001), 14.

15

BEING AS GIFT

Our penultimate day with the Kung Fu Pandas was, thanks be to God, uneventful. We had made arrangements to camp that night in a valley just to the east of Mount Yale. Being only several miles from an access point, the other half of the group (those who left after the first day) would be able to pack in. This allowed us to share our last evening together, drawing a tumultuous few days to a happy close. That being said, there is no easy day on the Colorado Trail. We still had seventeen miles of long sustained climbs through the Collegiate foothills that would accumulate to nearly 4,700 feet of elevation gain. By this point, the Pandas had shown the grit that we knew would see them through. Their final test of the day would be the last three miles, a stretch that would be arguably the steepest section of the entire trail.

Twenty years prior, nearly to the day, I had first passed through this wilderness beneath Mount Yale. Our climb that day is my earliest memory of the great confluence of my life—the love of the high peaks now brought to bear on the communion of love, which is the Church of Jesus Christ. After so many years marked by interior frustration and a quiet bitterness toward life, I found that the desire for the peaks and love of the backcountry did not need to be left behind to follow Jesus. In fact, the precise opposite was the case: new depths of the experience began to unfold. Mount Yale will forever testify to this: I remember every detail of that beautiful and sunny morning—the people I was with, the conversations we had, as if it were yesterday. Christian friendship, within the experience of the mountains, now revealed the new key to the interpretation of my life—that *being* is itself a gift.

"What constitutes the person", writes Giussani, "is a *given*; it is the product of another."[1] Despite the illusions of self-creation, deep down man senses that he did not make himself and is not in control of where he is going. For this reason, to be a human person is to be religious. But religion is a question, one that requires an answer. For the Christian, the answer is revelation—that God reveals himself in Jesus Christ. This does not eliminate the religious nature of Christianity, but it does transform it. In this sense, the Christian faith cannot be reduced to one of the many world religions. It stands alone, utterly and completely upon the testimony that God became man.

When Jesus reveals God as an eternal exchange of love, creation is reinterpreted as gift. He is the one sent by the Father, given to us through the Holy Spirit (cf. Heb 12:2). Within the Trinitarian life of God, we discover the origins of the gift of love. This illuminates the essence of created love, namely, that it has the structure of a gift. If God is the fullness of being and likewise the fullness of love, then we can arrive at a truly incredible conclusion: God is gift, and therefore all being is itself gift.

As we mentioned before, it has become customary to speak, not of creation, but of "nature". When we do this,

---

[1] L. Giussani, *The Risk of Education*, trans. Rosanna M. Giammanco (New York, Crossroad, 2001), 98.

we replace a relational term with a cold abstraction. Self-subsisting and autonomous, nature becomes something that is "just there", not something that came to be through the creative genius of love. It does not speak of love and no longer can be theologically interpreted. In the end, when we reduce all of creation to de-personalized nature, we lose its most precise core—that it is gift.

In his short book, *The Gift: Creation*, Kenneth Schmitz identifies this widespread attitude as a central stumbling block. "The chief obstacle to a better appreciation of the category of the gift", he writes, "is the attitude that takes the world as a *given fact*."[2] The scientific notion of nature is fact; the revelation of creation is gift. In a modern vision of reality, there is no verification of the giftedness of being—for the category itself is too expansive for the confines of the scientific method. Because the modern world is defined by a rejection of Christian revelation, so too is the category of gift first relegated to, and then eliminated from metaphysics. But despite this modern revaluation, deep within the human heart is the desire for gift. No matter their worldview, any honest souls cannot help but be moved by the fact that the mountains we see before us are gifts to which we owe gratitude. The problem is *to whom*—and herein lies the crisis of the age.

God created the world, not out of necessity, but out of the giftedness of his inner life and love. Gift then becomes the central lens for the Christian interpretation of reality. Though this may not make sense to the transactional world of adults, it is the most evident thing in the world to children. More than anything else, we express love in the form of gift and, by this, image the creativity of

[2] K. Schmitz, *The Gift: Creation* (Milwaukee: Marquette University Press, 1982), 34.

God in our gift-giving. Animals may signal and provide for one another; but only humans make gifts. Even more than this, we can say that not only do humans desire to make gifts, they cannot find themselves apart from gift giving. The Church beautifully described this at the Second Vatican Council as the law of self-gift: "Man, who is the only creature on earth which God willed for itself, cannot fully find himself except through a sincere gift of himself."[3]

As beautiful as the law of gift may be, attempting it in the reality of a fallen world brings serious frustration and a lot of pain. This is one reason why the framework of gift has fatigued and even atrophied in our modern world. What is required now is a reappraisal of this most innate mystery.

The law of the gift requires two things. First, to be a gift, it must be free. Gratuity is the hallmark of giftedness. If it is necessitated, it is a transaction and not a gift. Gifts are free endowments—free both in the giver and in the receiver. The second requirement of a gift is that it requires a response. When a gift is given, it is not completed until it is properly received. As Schmitz explains: "A gift is meant to be reciprocated. The fundamental reciprocity called for, however, is not the return of another gift. It is rather the completion of the gift being given.... Reception is the original reciprocity intended in the very meaning and reality of the gift. Receptivity on the part of the recipient is the primary requisite for the completion of the gift."[4]

Like all things, this mystery begins in God. If God is love and thereby the perfection of self-gift in eternal exchange,

---

[3] Second Vatican Council, Pastoral Constitution on the Church in the Modern World, *Gaudium et Spes* (December 7, 1965), no. 24.

[4] Schmitz, *The Gift*, 47.

then he is perfect and complete in himself. The Father, making a total gift of self to the Son from all eternity, is likewise eternally received and reciprocated by the Son and returned to the Father. The Third Person of the Trinity, the Holy Spirit, is the love itself—the gift of the giving Father and the receiving Son.

This is likewise manifested in creation. As a free gift and plan of sheer goodness, creation then requires reception. Does this necessitate God in order to complete creation? If that were the case, then he would need something, a violation of his perfection. The answer once again lies in the mystery of the Incarnation: God became man and, through his filial gift of self to the Father on the Cross, restores the gift-structure of creation to us, in his eternal act of reception. The Christian, then, has one task—to be drawn into Christ's receptive love of the Father by becoming sons and daughters in the Son. In Jesus' total gift of filial sonship, we find complete reception of the total gift.

The last of our steep trail followed the cascades of water flowing from the snowy heights of Mount Yale. Cresting the top of the switchbacks, we finally passed through the trees and gained our first glimpse of the mountain. The valley before us expanded westward and then, suddenly, went vertically to the heights.

Reentering the woods on the north side of the basin, we were greeted by cheers and elation: the group we had left at the Twin Lakes had safely arrived from their detour. Gathering around their fire, we assessed the state of the weather to decide how and where we would say Mass. Sensing an onslaught of rain likely to come during Mass, we decided nonetheless to do it outdoors. The only other option was to try to get fourteen of us into my four-man tent. And frankly, the smell of the Pandas ruled out this possibility almost immediately.

After the Mass in the rainstorm, I looked and saw Cody and Casey out in the meadow. They stood looking far above treeline, once again in debate. We had all been surprised that after two weeks in the backcountry, we had not seen mountain goats—until now. I watched the customary shaking of hands as they entered into the latest bet; Cody with total assurance that those tiny white dots on the mountainside were goats; Casey with the cool collectivity that they were, once again, just rocks. After an impressive thirty-minute showdown, the "goats" had not moved, and Cody once again conceded to losing another bet. At the rate he was losing, Cody would be buying Casey a daily beer for the rest of his life. Perhaps in time, the harsh transactional nature of Cody's bet would be softened by the gift of Casey's mercy. But for now, it was clear, he was going to hold it over his head.

16

A PILGRIMAGE TO BEAUTY

The sun had yet to break as we crested the pass south of Mount Yale, which began our descent toward Rainbow Lake. The Pandas were refreshed from the cool night's sleep, reinvigorated by the anticipated arrival at Mount Princeton Hot Springs—their departure and our resupply stop. But before all that, we had another sixteen miles of circumnavigating the peak named after Princeton University.

During the mid-1800s, survey teams were sent from the major universities of the East to begin articulating the contours of the expansive, and largely unknown, American West. It was for this reason that the Collegiate Peaks got their names—Yale, Harvard, Columbia, Oxford, and Princeton, to name a few. We had spent the last four days traversing these giants on their eastern side and would still have another two days before leaving the Collegiate Peaks of the Sawatch Range.

But for now, our minds were occupied with only one thought—reaching the Mount Princeton Hot Springs. We started early, knowing it was going to be hot today. The resilience of the Pandas began to wane, but so too did the hardened veneer of my trusted lieutenants. Looking back over the group, I saw Cody, Casey, and Luke in deep conversation with the young men, bringing them hope and encouragement.

As a college chaplain in Boulder, I started an outdoor club called Aquinas Alpine. The purpose? To take young people into places of unspeakable beauty in the hope that it would rekindle their desire for God. We ascended the peaks of Colorado, descended the slot canyons of Utah, and spent many hours traversing snowy winter routes to backcountry huts.

Reflecting on the experience of those two years, I now see what it really was—a shared pilgrimage, walking toward a spiritual destination. In the Middle Ages, Christians were steeped in this vision of spiritual pilgrimage; the three greatest being the journey to Rome, Jerusalem, and Santiago de Compostelo (northwestern Spain). As my time in Boulder drew to a close, I wanted to take the students on a pilgrimage—but not necessarily to a place. Though our destination was to be Switzerland (that which no greater beauty can be conceivable), it was in fact *a pilgrimage to beauty*. The criteria were threefold; we would hike each day to the huts above treeline, hear conferences on beauty by Father Gawronski, and drink the finest German beer the huts could afford. And we set off—all thirty-seven of us—toward the heights of beauty.

In 1961, Hans Urs von Balthasar began writing his sixteen-volume magnus opus known as the Trilogy. Over the next twenty-six years, he would complete the three-part work on the confrontation of the transcendentals with Divine Revelation, respectively called the theological aesthetics, dramatics, and logic. In other words, von Balthasar would take truth, goodness, and beauty—what Plato called the three attributes of all being (i.e., transcendentals)—and reflect on them in light of God's self-disclosure in Jesus

Christ. How did God reveal himself as the fullness of uncreated truth, goodness, and beauty and thereby refashion our experience of their created forms? The Trilogy, a work of massive scope and profound insight, is one of the great theological achievements of the last century—one that we will be unpacking for centuries to come. But for our purposes and that of my pilgrimage, what is most interesting was his method.

"Beauty is the word that shall be our first", he wrote at the beginning of the Trilogy.[1] This is striking, because the typical way of speaking about transcendentals is first truth, then goodness, and last of all, beauty. Von Balthasar, seeing how the dictatorship of relativism had barred modern man from engaging claims of the eternal nature of truths, as well as the moral dimension of goodness, proposed a different method. Start with beauty, that thing which modern man still perceives and is enraptured by; and from it will come the desire to be good and, thereby, a new openness to the truth. Perhaps von Balthasar knew this from his days as a chaplain at the University of Basel. For my part, I knew it was precisely the method needed at the University of Colorado.

Beauty moves us in ways we don't understand. In fact, we often don't even realize that we are moving. To explain this, von Balthasar cites the poet Rilke: "There is no place in it which does not see you. You must change your life."[2] In the experience of beauty, man is moved to goodness; for beauty always demands an ethical response. But what is it that moves us? Beauty is not just in the eye of the beholder; it is first of all in the object itself. In the intersection between the objective and subjective dimensions of beauty, we discover the essence of the

---

[1] H. U. von Balthasar, *The Glory of the Lord: A Theological Aesthetics*, vol. 1, *Seeing the Form*, trans. Erasmo Leiva-Merikakis, 2nd ed. (San Francisco: Ignatius Press, 2009), 18.

[2] Ibid., 23.

beautiful—what the Germans call *Gestalt*. "The beautiful is above all a *form* (*Gestalt*), and the light does not fall on this form from above and from outside, rather it breaks forth from the form's interior.... Visible form not only 'points' to an invisible, unfathomable mystery; form is the apparition of this mystery, and reveals it while, naturally, at the same time protecting and veiling it."[3]

The thing is beautiful in itself, because it has a *Gestalt* (an untranslatable German word meaning form, figure, or shape). Be it a beautiful woman, a Caravaggio in the Vatican Museum, or a picturesque mountain landscape, beauty is first and foremost in the thing itself—precisely as a form. Saint Thomas Aquinas described this objective dimension as the intersection between *species* and *lumen*, form and splendor. The beautiful object is, as von Balthasar continues, "the real presence ... *and* ... a real pointing".[4] In addition to this, Immanuel Kant worked out a subjective dimension, a complementary structure that reflects not only the object itself but how man perceives it. This he describes as two moments: the encounter with beauty is first a "beholding", and then a being "enraptured". No one can really behold who has not also been enraptured, and no one can be enraptured who has not already perceived. In all this, we are seeking to expand modern man's vision of reality, first by complementing the vision of the true and the good with that of the beautiful. Dante knew this, when he described the experience of Purgatory as "*d'ire a farsi belle*" ("that they must go to beautify themselves").[5] The whole of the Christian life is about being made beautiful—but beautiful according to and within the form of beauty itself, the God-man, Jesus Christ.

[3] Ibid., 146–47.
[4] Ibid., 116.
[5] Dante, *Purgatorio*, Canto 18:74.

But to live the experience of beauty requires that we learn how to see again. In the fifth century b.c., a philosopher named Anaxagoras was asked the question "Why are we here on earth?" His answer: "To behold." Since that time, the Western philosophical tradition has always affirmed this "beholding" to be the most noble and important of human acts.

What I had learned in my time as a college chaplain was that the students were afflicted by a crisis of perception. The technocratic and activistic world, in which they were immersed, rendered the ability to behold beauty nearly impossible. What was necessary was to recreate the circumstances where this spiritual posture would again become possible. And there was no other place than the serene and undeniable beauty of creation. As von Balthasar affirms: "It isn't right that we should have to overlook the beauty ... of the world in order to love God in them. The lover finds his beloved's house and garden all the lovelier when she is present in them: he loves them for his beloved's sake, and his beloved in them, and he is not blind to anything that relates to her."[6] When we are immersed in the beauty of creation, only one thing remains: to discover the beauty behind all beauty, namely, God. As beauty itself, when one possesses him, he possesses all beauty.

Feet were drawing flame as we gradually made our way upon those last few miles to the hot springs. While the agony of anticipation pitched, something remarkable and unexpected occurred: we thru-hikers realized that we were actually going to miss the Kung Fu Pandas. Just as the absence of a pre-frontal cortex made them the most ridiculous of

---

[6]H.U. von Balthasar, *The Grain of Wheat: Aphorisms*, trans. Erasmo Leiva-Merikakis (San Francisco: Ignatius Press, 2011), 98.

trail companions, their grit and hard-fought character made them the most endearing. And I was reminded of a line from Chesterton that would summarize our days together, and, in fact, the entire Colorado Trail. "It is when you have groups of men chosen irrationally that you have men. The element of adventure begins to exist; for an adventure is, by its nature, a thing that comes to us. It is a thing that chooses us, not a thing that we choose."[7]

Something of the "irrationality" of the collection of groups on the trail made for an element of unexpected adventure. The Kung Fu Pandas had been drama since the second they stepped on the trail. In contrast, my thru-hiking companions—Luke, Cody, and Casey—now 170 miles into the trail, were strong and galvanized. We could have completed the thru-hike with minimal drama and no headaches were we not to take on these other groups. But now, we were starting to love the human aspect of the adventure, of challenging young men to pass beyond their mental and physical limits, acquiring a new and unforeseen self-confidence.

We bid farewell to the Kung Fu Pandas and made our way to the longed-for hot springs. But the soak was quickly interrupted—the new recruits had arrived, with their oversized bags and adolescent bravado. A car full of them passed, with heads hanging out the windows like derping corgis. Cody and Casey stood by with resting faces of utter disbelief. What would tomorrow bring? No one knew for sure. It would likely be an irrational collection of men on adventure—and it would be beautiful.

---

[7] G. K. Chesterton, "Heretics", in *The Collected Works of G. K. Chesterton*, vol. 1 (San Francisco: Ignatius Press, 1986), 142.

17

LASCIATE OGNE SPERANZA

Far below treeline, our new group, the Derping Corgis, passed joyfully through a forest of lodgepole pines. We had left Mount Princeton Hot Springs at sunrise and began our eastward traverse around the last few peaks of the southern Sawatch Range. Looking up to the west, I could see Antero, the mountain under which we were passing.

I love mountains, but I've never liked Mount Antero. Not that it is the mountain's fault—it's just a big, ugly, pile of rocks. But in May of 2002, during the last days of my senior year in high school, I made a fateful and reckless attempt at its summit that should have ended my life.

After a first period, a buddy and I decided to skip the rest of the day and head to climb Antero—a two-hour drive from Denver. This means that we were starting up the peak around 11 a.m., the typical time when you should be descending. But we were eighteen and, to the best of our knowledge, indestructible.

As we reached the saddle, a typical early season snowstorm started to roll in. I distinctly remember passing climbers begging us to descend. But we continued to climb, not realizing the impending peril. As we reached the summit, lightning struck on the far side of the summit, twenty feet away. The thunder that erupted from that proximity was unlike anything I have ever experienced. Static electricity surged through the air, and the very metal in my boots began to shock my feet. As the snow and wind crashed against the mountainside, we ran desperately down the side of the peak. The lightning continued to crack as if a whip were driving us from the mountain. It was a moment of absolute powerlessness, of total and complete fear. It was nothing short of Hell.

Hell is something we moderns rarely speak of. In a world where "everyone is nice", the thought of a place of eternal damnation seems as illusory as it does absurd. But Hell is part of creation and is a real possibility, an essential part of Christian consciousness. It stands in a logical connection to the reality of sin and to the historical event known as "the Fall". The concept of salvation stands only with the accepted fact that we need to be saved from something.

Modernity's denial of Hell is intimately tied to the belief that sin does not exist and salvation is not necessary. But has it made the world a better place? Joseph Ratzinger says otherwise: "In our age, which has removed anxiety about salvation and sin from man and has thus apparently made him free from fear, these new anxieties are rampant and often take on the form of collective psychoses ... all these anxieties are masks for fear of death, alarm at the finiteness of our being."[1]

What, then, is Hell? As my experience on Antero can relay, Hell begins when we assert ourselves as God—the sovereign ruler of our own destiny. It implies the rejection of God—and, thereby, the rejection of creatureliness. Within this is the rejection of relationship, of dependence,

[1] J. Ratzinger, *The Yes of Jesus Christ: Exercises in Faith, Hope, and Love*, trans. Robert Nowell (New York: Crossroad, 2016), 85.

and all limitations. It is the destination for the one who takes the Nietzschean path "to go it alone". Or in the words sung by Frank Sinatra, "I did it my way." As the author Sigrid Undset describes, the path to Heaven or Hell is the fundamental decision of every human being: "Either he will isolate himself in himself and the Hell of egotism, or will give himself over to God in power and be freed from the cage of ego worship and to eternal possibilities."[2] We can describe this in three ways.

First, Hell is the nullification of faith. In its essence, faith is the ability to trust in relationship, a decidedly human act. It provides a kind of relational way of knowing, one that is indispensable for human life. As Giussani writes, "the more one is truly human, the more one is able to trust, because he understands the reasons for believing in another."[3] It is upon these natural grounds that God builds up the supernatural act of faith in relationship to Jesus Christ. If we reject this, we commit to viewing the world as fundamentally untrustworthy. If Hell is the place whereby trust is abolished, then relationship remains the absolute obstacle. The words of the existentialist philosopher Sartre now ring true: "Hell is other people."[4] This devastating conclusion is as consistent as it is compelling. If I am the center of my own self-actualizing being and the sole interpreter of reality, then anyone who impedes this is the problem.

Second, Hell is a place of total hopelessness. No image will ever capture this as powerfully as when Dante is led by Virgil through the gates of Hell in the opening cantos

---

[2] S. Undset, "My Reasons to Convert", in S. Jaki, *Sigrid Undset's Quest for Truth* (Port Huron: Real View Books, 2007), 289.

[3] L. Giussani, *The Religious Sense*, trans. John Zucchi (Montreal: McGill-Queen's University Press, 1998), 20.

[4] J. P. Sartre, *No Exit*, in *No Exit and Three Other Plays* (New York: Vintage Books, 1946), 47.

of the *Inferno*. There, Dante reads upon the entryway: "*Lasciate ogne speranza, voi ch'entrate*": "Abandon all hope, ye who enter."[5] Hope, the great virtue of the pilgrimage through life, ceases to exist in the place of total damnation. But it begins in this life—for to live without hope is to live in Hell. We forget the catastrophic effects of sin, how they paralyze us in a state of confusion. Far too often, the hopelessness of modern man is built on the ruined dreams of a bourgeois paradise. By this I mean that in our day, we have supplanted the Gospel of Jesus Christ with an intra-worldly vision of a total happiness in this life, attained through the possession of affluence, comfort, and well-being. When our hope lies in the materialistic auto-salvation of the moment, we soon find ourselves in the depths of personal Hell.

Third and most profoundly, Hell is the abolition of love. In Dostoevsky's *Brothers Karamazov*, we hear the Elder Zosima offer these words: "I ask myself: 'What is hell?' And I answer thus: 'The suffering of being no longer able to love.'"[6] We often think of the opposite of love being hate; but returning to the imagery of Dante, it is in fact pride, and not hatred, that opposes love. The depths of Hell are frozen in the ice of loveless pride. And while hatred (or wrath) is indeed a damnable offense, the death of the heart in pride is the true center of Hell.

Love flows from the heart of man, as the deepest expression of his inner self. The heart then, as the psychic center of man's rationality and affectivity, determines the trajectory of his loves, by either ordering them rightly or inordinately according to the reality of things. So often, we

---

[5] Dante, *Inferno*, 3:3.

[6] F. Dostoevsky, *The Brothers Karamazov*, trans. Richard Pevear and Larissa Volokhonsky (New York: Everyman's Library, 1992), 322.

love things with great excess or defect, leading the heart to atrophy or hypertropy. We can't seem to get the loves of this life right and thus end up in self-enclosed caverns—places without love.

How then are we to avoid the tyranny of Hell? We must undergo a transformation of the heart by loving all things in God. As Dietrich von Hildebrand eloquently explains:

> It is rather the *amare in Deo*, "the loving all things in God," which here marks the transformation of our heart. This attitude implies not only that we love Christ above all, but also that our love of all other things is incorporated in Christ. Thus, for example, beauty in nature and art should be enjoyed in Christ. This does not mean that we should consider the beauty in question only as a starting point for meditation about Christ. It means rather that this fully appreciated beauty draws us *in conspectu Dei*, that we find in its own quality a ray of God's infinite beauty, and that we hear in it the voice of Christ.[7]

Mount Antero remains, to this day, the place where I experienced Hell—and very likely could have been sent. I was led there in my naïve rejection of creatureliness; and I experienced it as chaos, void of trusting faith, abiding hope, and confident love. But it was, thanks be to God, not to be my end.

We concluded another eighteen-mile day at a pleasant, streamside campsite at the foot of Mount Shavano. Antero was behind us, and the pack of wild, young corgis sat derping on a log waiting for Mass. Casey, who had become our medic, was doing his usual round of triage work

---

[7] D. von Hildebrand, *The Heart* (South Bend: St. Augustine's Press, 2007), 124.

on the day's blisters. "Your boots are a disgrace", I over-heard him say to one of them, "and your socks are even worse." Accustomed as we were to ill-preparation, this was a new level.

I dreamed that night of Antero—but it was different. The dawn broke as we crested the mountain summit, and, in an instant, the tears and soot from that hellish storm were wiped away by the cool breeze of fresh morning air. It was the peace of God, known only by his presence. Waking from the dream, I resolved never again to live in Hell and to begin again the work of loving all things in God.

18

LIVE IN THE IS

I woke, just before 4 a.m., to the smell of Nutella. Luke, Cody, and Casey, my tentmates for the month, were still sound asleep. Opening the vestibule of the tent, I was horrified to find a container of Europe's favorite hazelnut cocoa spread left open throughout the night. Surely this was not intentional? I knew that Casey and Cody were disappointed not to have encountered a bear and that Casey hadn't carried a handgun all this way just for looks. But this was the next level—they were baiting a bear into our tent with an open container of Nutella.

We roused the Corgis from their puppyish slumber and began our preparations for the day. I was filled with excitement: today would be a watershed moment on the trail. The next seventeen miles were the last march across the seemingly never-ending Sawatch Range, concluding with our ascent of Marshall Pass. From here I knew that we would look out and see, far to the west, San Luis Peak—the sentinel entryway to the San Juan Mountains and the last frontier of the Colorado Trail.

The first hours of the day were calm and steady. But as we approached treeline, we looked up toward the pass and saw a trail pitching to steeper and steeper grades, before dissolving into the sky. The pain of prior miles was accumulating, and we roused the men to take heart. I knew that if we could just get them over the pass, they would all make it to Crested Butte—because that night, they were going to get ambushed.

The trail, not the hiker, determines the shape of the hike. Certainly, we choose specific routes for particular reasons; but once you set onto the trail, its contour is what is ultimately determinative. In this sense, one of the key virtues of any student of the backcountry is receptivity. In the mountains, very little is in your control—the trail leads you up this or that pass, the weather turns and soaks you to the core, animals come and go according to their own instinct. Your first task is to receive.

Father Gawronski had an axiom that he would often tell me: "Live in the is, not in the ought." What he meant by this was to receive things as they come, and then do what presents itself. One of the greatest temptations in the Christian life is to reduce it to a kind of moralism; a system of "oughts and shoulds". Yes, life should look differently; I ought to be better, etc. But so much of freedom and wholeness arises out of the stance of self-acceptance, which is only acquired within the spiritual posture of receptivity before creation.

Now receptivity is not passivity—it is a form of action. In this way, we can speak of it (albeit delicately) in reference to the God who is pure act. Whenever Jesus turns and speaks to the Father, we see his posture of total receptivity mysteriously reverberating throughout creation. "I thank you, Father, Lord of heaven and earth, that you have hidden these things from the wise and understanding and revealed them to infants; yes, Father, for such was your gracious will. All things have been delivered to me by my Father" (Mt 11:25–26).

The filial pattern of Christ's existence is marked by this eternal reception of his sonship from the Father. This is the hidden meaning of "all things have been delivered to me." Jesus' life, lived totally from the Father, means that he receives everything from him, perfectly and completely in the moment. Undercutting the pharisaic project of moralism, the Son's perfect obedience to the Father opened up an entirely new religious disposition. As Romano Guardini describes:

> The fundamental attitude of Jesus' life develops in this atmosphere of openness: His readiness to accept and accomplish what the hour brings, His obedience to the Father's will.... His approach brings men fundamentally to Himself in their true Being and He further encourages them to reveal their true selves. A man is determined by the attitude he adopts towards Christ.[1]

"Living in the is" can be called openness, readiness, or receptivity. It is always, nonetheless, a hallmark of life in Christ. This is exemplified in the life of Mary, the purest Christian form, who models it in the feminine posture of total receptivity. Through it, God becomes man, and she, the pattern of the Church at prayer. As Mary mirrors and images her Son, we come to understand that "the only meaningful attitude is a readiness to encounter that which is."[2]

This posture of receptivity is so foreign to the American mentality of "do it yourself activism" that we really don't have a word for it. In Italy, they speak of *disponibilità*

---

[1] R. Guardini, *Freedom, Grace, and Destiny: Three Chapters in the Interpretation of Existence*, trans. John Murray, S.J. (New York: Pantheon Books, 1961), 198.

[2] R. Guardini as quoted in H.U. von Balthasar, *Romano Guardini: Reform from the Source*, trans. Albert K. Wimmer and D.C. Schindler (San Francisco: Ignatius Press, 2010), 90.

(likewise, in the French *disponibilité*). The closest rendering in our language would be "disponibility"—letting oneself be disposed. It means releasing the clinched hands of control and surrendering to the reality of things. It requires me to renounce my self-constructed pattern of life and all inordinate preoccupations. When life appears to be "as it shouldn't be" and the trail takes a turn that I don't want, I can choose to be disponible. This is the receptive posture of Mary, who simply lets things be. In the words of von Balthasar, "the perfection of man means simply: being open for the mystery, being available for God, for his grace, for being claimed ever anew, for mission."[3] And this radically recasts how we think of perfection and holiness.

It's easy to speak of these things in the abstract; it is in the arena of human relationships that it gets more complicated. I remember a climb on the Zugspitze, the highest peak in Germany, where this was made clear. Packing into the hut the day before with my friend, we set out that morning toward the vertical heights of the mountain's north face. Fortunately, it was a *via ferrata* route, where you clip your harness into anchors bolted on the cliff. When we approached the first pitch, I said to him, "Let's get our harnesses on", to which he replied sternly, "You never told me to bring my harness." You can imagine how the conversation ensued. But the simple fact was that it was too dangerous to downclimb, and that we had to climb the face and share the harness. It was a moment that required both of us to receive the circumstances as they came, though they were totally undesirable. In moments like these, I always appreciate the words of Pier Giorgio Frassati, who could also draw out the comedic in such complicated situations: "The outing was marvelous in

[3] H. U. von Balthasar, "Spirit and Fire: An Interview with Hans Urs von Balthasar", in *Communio* 32 (Fall 2005): 587.

general, but very difficult; we ... missed the ladies, but in the end, we were glad not to have had them along, because otherwise we would have involuntarily exposed them to some very raw emotions."[4]

As ridiculous as the climb on the *Zugspitze* may have been, it demonstrates the great challenge of learning to love by receiving things as they are. It's hardest with ourselves: this is why self-acceptance stands at the center between self-knowledge and self-gift. But this is the only route toward fulfillment—being loved for who we are and not what we should be. For this reason, Giussani calls self-acceptance "the essential characteristic of the human being".[5]

But lest this take an excessively therapeutic turn, the path of self-acceptance follows from the acceptance of a deeper truth—that I am *from* the other. This deepest of relationships, one that goes to the very core of my being, is how I learn truly to receive myself. Only then can it be reinforced by others, where we learn the relational art form that "blends indetermination with readiness".[6] The depths of my being are not determined by me; I therefore begin again with a readiness to receive.

Buried within the mountainous corpus of Hans Urs von Balthasar, there is a thread of this theme, which he calls *Mitsein*. From the German *mit* ("with") and *sein* ("being"), *Mitsein* simply means "being with". For von Balthasar, "to be" is always "to be with". This is a provocative antidote to the modern spirit of radical and autonomous individualism. This metaphysically begins in God, the creator of human life, whose being sustains all being. But existentially, it began even before we were conscious—as our

[4] P. G. Frassati, *Letters to His Friends and Family*, trans. Timothy E. Deeter (Ann Arbor: Alba House, 2009), 201.

[5] L. Giussani, *The Religious Sense*, trans. John Zucchi (Montreal: McGill-Queen's University Press, 1998), 97.

[6] Guardini, *Freedom, Grace, and Destiny*, 107.

mother lovingly gazed upon us and awakened us to being. As von Balthasar writes:

> The developing human being (once more in contrast to the animal) is intrinsically ordered to "being *with*" [*Mitsein*] other men, so much so that he awakens to self-consciousness only through other human beings, normally through his mother. In the mother's smile, it dawns on him that there is a world into which he is accepted and in which he is welcome, and it is in this primordial experience that he becomes aware of himself for the first time. This [is the] founding event of human existence.... Long before the child learns to speak, a mute dialogue unfolds between mother and child on the basis of the "being with" that is constitutive of every conscious human being.[7]

When the founding event of human existence is love, then we find ourselves in a world where it is safe to receive. Self-consciousness, self-expression, and self-awareness begin, not in the self, but in the prior act of being received. And when that other is love, we begin the adventure of human life with the confidence that the reality of things is in fact good. From here we can affirm with Joseph Ratzinger a basic principle of human life:

> Man comes in the most profound sense to himself, not through what he does, but through what he accepts. He must wait for the gift of love, and love can only be received as a gift. It cannot be "made" on one's own, without anyone else; one must wait for it, let it be given to one. And one cannot become *wholly* man in any other

[7]J. Ratzinger and H. U. von Balthasar, *Mary: The Church at the Source*, trans. Adrian Walker (San Francisco: Ignatius Press, 2005), 102–3. Cf. H. U. von Balthasar, *Explorations in Theology*, vol. 3, *Creator Spirit*, trans. Brian McNeil, C.R.V. (San Francisco: Ignatius Press, 1993), 16.

way than by being loved, by letting oneself be loved. That love represents simultaneously both man's highest possibility and his deepest need and that this most necessary thing is at the same time the freest and the most unenforceable means precisely that for his "salvation" man is meant to rely on receiving.[8]

This opens us to the deeper horizons of human existence and to the reality of God himself. In the end, it is Jesus Christ who receives us, in all our brokenness and sin, into the heart of the Father.

Our camp that evening looked like a Corgi battlefield. Bodies were everywhere, laid out in a state of total exhaustion. Not only were tents not set, they were lying on the ground with their packs still on. Even when a mother moose and her calf entered our camp, the pups were unfazed.

Suddenly a black Jeep pulled into the camp—the ambush was right on time. Knowing that our next 100 miles were nowhere near an exit point or possible resupply, I had arranged with my friend Tom to come from Crested Butte and to ambush our crew with a pizza delivery. The Corgis were like men in a dream, and the pizza was not consumed, but annihilated. But the joys of that night would remain some of the greatest of the trail—all thanks to Tom and some underserved hospitality. Today we would sleep with full stomachs and an even fuller sense of accomplishment. The Sawatch were behind us, Marshall Pass below us—and it was time to turn westward and make for the Cochetopa Hills.

[8] J. Ratzinger, *Introduction to Christianity*, trans. J. R. Foster (San Francisco: Ignatius Press, 2004), 267.

19

THE RELEVANCE OF THE STARS

Our passage through Marshall Pass brought us into "no-man's land". The Cochetopa Hills (named after the Ute Indian word for "buffalo") were arid and uninspiring. We rolled steadily along forested hilltops diseased by the mountain pine beetle—that arborous cancer all too familiar to Coloradans. But our climbing was not finished, for the day would conclude at the top of Sargents Mesa. This high mountain clearing, situated at the center of the Sawatch, Sangre de Cristo, and San Juan mountains, would offer a most expansive view in every direction. That morning, like most, began under starlight. And glancing upward, I was transported back two decades, to the most beautiful time I have ever seen the stars.

It was the summer of 2005, and I was climbing Mount Rainier in Washington. The mountain, though being the height of a Colorado fourteener, is an active volcano covered in glaciers. With twenty-six named glaciers and over fifty unnamed, the peak requires you to start your ascent 10,000 feet below the summit (twice the gain of most Colorado peaks). After a long day, ascending the first half of the elevation in white-out conditions, we arrived at Camp Muir. Situated two miles above sea level, just below the serious glacial climbing, we ate some food and crawled into our sleeping bags.

At midnight we woke and began our preparations for the ascent. I looked up the immense mountainside before us; the moon had set, and the stars were radiant and totally clear. Upon the subtle glow of Rainier's glaciated face, I could see climbers before us, making their way through a maze of crevices. Their headlamps traced a vertical line up thousands of feet until they blended into the stars above. To this day, I don't know where the light of climbers ended and the lamps of Heaven began.

In the ancient world, the stars navigated life on earth. Our ancestors, living in a pre-industrial world, were attentive to them in a way that we moderns don't understand. This is evidenced by how we speak; what they called "the heavens" we now call "space". When Dante climbed out of Hell, he wasn't looking at space—he was beholding the Heavens.

> He first and I behind, we climbed so high
> that through a small round opening I saw
> some of the turning beauties of the sky,
> And we came out to see, once more, the stars.[1]

The stars not only express the astonishing grandeur of creation; they give praise to the infinitude of God. As long as he has walked the earth, man has looked up at the stars and seen in them his own desire for transcendence. Their majestic expanse awakens in the human heart its own desire for more than the finite and limited things of this life—that a mystery lies just beyond the grasp of our concepts and that we are made to move beyond the confines of our own understanding and knowledge. In other words,

[1] Dante, *Inferno*, Canto 34.

the stars remind us that we are made for the infinite, made for transcendence—and that nothing finite can satisfy the human heart.

The first task of the Christian in the postmodern age is to get people looking at the stars. By turning off the screens and looking upward, we have to begin asking the question again of how this corresponds to the desires of our hearts. Only then will we be reawakened to the experience of being truly human. We need to help people understand that what they are looking at is not just the "universe", but what the Greeks called *kosmos*. The original use of the word comes from Pythagoras, who described it as a harmonious order. The stars speak of this rational arrangement of reality, that things are not random or absurd. And from the intelligibility of the rational order, I can derive a sense of my own destiny, that it is in fact reasonable to believe and follow. This is the lesson of the stars.

A most unusual story is told of the young Father Luigi Giussani. Biking through the streets of Milan one evening, he stopped to see a couple making out in the park. He abruptly stopped them and said, "What does what you are doing have to do with the stars?" Then he biked away. You can imagine their awkward astonishment. But the question had been posed—how are the stars relevant to the love you are seeking? How do they elicit the desires of the heart? And are you living your desires in relation to them and to the transcendence they call for? It was a stroke of brilliance from an idiosyncratic young priest.

But looking up at the stars is just the beginning. We need to be reeducated in why I desire to transcend the known world, to seek the mystery beyond all things. Here, Giussani provides a most powerful educational method, calling it *the religious sense*.

Contrary to the modern, rationalistic idea that religion belongs to a kind of superstitious emotionalism, Giussani proposes anew that religion is not elective, but structural to human existence. To be religious is to be human, because it is a sense within the person that makes him capable of self-transcendence (i.e., interested in the stars). All this talk of "I'm spiritual and not religious" describes a fundamental, anthropological error. Religion is innate to our human nature, configuring the way we encounter the world. Any person who is truly and humanly alive lives religiously, coming to see the world according to its full breadth.

As we spoke of earlier on the trail, it was Luigi Giussani who has helped us rediscover the idea that religion is a *sense*. And the key to understanding it as such is its relationship to reason. "The religious sense", Giussani writes, "is reason's capacity to express its own profound nature in the ultimate question."[2] This sense, which is reasonable, opens man to the possibility of faith in Jesus Christ. But in order to make this possible, we have to expand our definition of reason, restoring it to its full and proper form. Reason is then, according to Giussani, "openness to reality, a capacity to seize and affirm it in all of its factors".[3] Contrary to the vision of modern rationalism, reason is not a piece of scientific machinery, existing for the production of deductive conclusions. It is the deepest thing in man, an intuitive sense of the heart that is profoundly and completely in accord with rationality. Only man's religious sense affords reason the capacity to "express its own profound nature in the ultimate question".[4] And in addition to defending the expansiveness

---

[2] L. Giussani, *The Religious Sense*, trans. John Zucchi (Montreal: McGill-Queen's University Press, 1998), 56.

[3] Ibid., 16.

[4] Ibid., 56.

of reason, we must again affirm the reasonableness of faith. If faith is in fact reasonable, then "prayer is the most rational act a human person can engage in."[5] Prayer becomes, as one theologian writes, "not a subjective and superficial piety ... but the constitutive substance of the rational act."[6]

This all begins by looking up at the stars. Our hearts are made for a mystery that transcends us, one that we know in Christ to be the living God. The religious sense, by awakening our hearts and bidding us upward, spurs on reason's climb to the summit of mystery. If we are to offer anything to modern man, we have first to be lovers of mystery. We have to show how our climbs and our every pursuit of the mountain heights of reason, all our desperate attempts at a Christological interpretation of the joys and sufferings of life, ultimately terminate at the summit and the perception of mystery. Then, we will look up at the stars and not know where the lights of human intelligence blend into the luminous brilliance of the mystery beyond.

Arriving at Sargents Mesa, we quickly realized we had no access to water. None whatsoever. The guidebook told us that a drought was coming—but I didn't realize how desperate it would be. As Luke and I prodded the Corgis up the final pitch to the Mesa's summit, I sent Cody and Casey to scout for water. When we met them at the top, their faces were clearly troubled. "The good news", they told me, "is that we found water; the bad news—it's a cattle trough." This would certainly test the quality of our purifiers and the constitution of our stomachs.

<hr />

[5] L. Chapp, *Confession of a Catholic Worker: Our Moment of Christian Witness* (San Francisco: Ignatius Press, 2023), 87.
[6] Ibid.

But we had little time to be preoccupied with the water quality on the Mesa—for that evening, we watched as a black wall of meteorological death made its way toward us from the west. Camped on the top of the Mesa, we would be the victims of whatever assault it would bring. In the last minutes before the storm broke, I saw the Corgis excitedly sitting outside their tents, bracing for the inevitable. All I could do was mentally rehearse what I was going to say to their parents. Cracks of thunder echoed throughout the Mesa as the assault began. The rains came in torrential form. All we could do was huddle in our tents, pray, and wait.

But like all things, the black wall passed the Mesa and fell eastward into the San Luis Valley. Night came, the clouds cleared, and we looked up once again to behold the stars.

20

BECAUSE IT'S THERE

As morning light dawned upon the Mesa, we started to survey the effects of the evening tempest. The cows were nowhere to be found, the ground was saturated, and even a few trees were down. But what was most incredible was the news we received from another thru-hiker, just a mile down the road. Lightning had struck a tree not twenty feet away from him, nearly setting his tent ablaze. He had a wild look in his eye as he conveyed the story of how he was able to put out the fire. We refilled his water and set out on our way. But we would meet this wild-eyed character again before the trail's end.

Twenty-one miles and 3,600 feet stood between us and Highway 114—our most anticipated resupply point of the entire month. For reaching that exit point of the trail, we would be lifted, as by angels, to the paradisal town of Crested Butte. Here we would celebrate in the company of friends and take our second and final rest day. From there we would garner the strength to prepare for the final and greatest feat of our month's adventure—the passage through the San Juans.

In 1923, the famed British climber George Mallory was asked by reporters why he was attempting to climb Mount

Everest, which at the time, had not been summited. And his answer became one of the most acclaimed and memorable in climbing history. "Because it's there ... Everest is the highest mountain in the world, and no man has reached its summit. Its existence is a challenge. The answer is instinctive, a part, I suppose, of man's desire to conquer the universe."[1]

The answer is telling of the *ethos* of mountaineering, especially during that romantic era of the early twentieth century. "Because it's there", I have a mandate to climb it. In other words, the existence of the peak requires of me an attempt at its summit. Why again? Because "of man's desire to conquer the universe". Mallory, a product of the modern age, sees the conquest of nature as the central reason for why we climb. It's the same spirit we bring to the Colorado Trail, the parlance of "bagging fourteeners" (a terrible term) or any mountain adventure, when we view the primary purpose for the mountain's existence as an exigency for man's conquest. But this instinctive drive, as it so often does, ended in tragedy: George Mallory and his companion froze to death on the side of Mount Everest—and it will never be known whether they in fact stood at the summit.

Thirty years later, a man named Edmund Hillary and his companion, Tenzing Norgay, became the first men to summit verifiably the highest peak in the world. Though Hillary and Norgay were likely drawn to climb Everest "because it was there", their rationale around climbing expressed a more profound vision of why we climb. As Hillary famously said, "It's not the mountains that we conquer, but ourselves."[2] A shift has occurred: the primary

---

[1] Cf. P. Gillman, *Wildest Dream: The Biography of George Mallory* (Seattle: Mountaineering Books, 2000), 222.

[2] Cf. M. Gill, *Edmund Hillary—A Biography* (Sheffield: Vertebrate Publishing, 2019).

drive to the summit is not the conquest of nature but the conquest of self. The nineteenth century, one filled with the obsessive conquest of the natural world, was giving way to the more existentialist vision of self-actualization.

Men like Hillary and Norgay were heroic in their undertaking and thoughtful in their reasoning. But when a Christian hears "because it's there", it strikes them in a deeper way. As we have said throughout these letters, the givenness of creation is due to the gratuitous love of the Creator; and this evidences a deeper logic than the conquest of nature and self. "Because they are there", the peaks call us to climb, not for themselves, but for the conquest of a deeper love.

Returning to Hillary's vision, the conquest of self is intrinsic to the Christian life—we call it *askesis*, or asceticism. In the Incarnational vision of reality, man is made to enter into the life of Christ, who became man in order to redeem us from the slavery of sin. Thus we enter into Christ only through the death of self: "If any man would come after me, let him deny himself and take up his cross and follow me" (Mt 16:24). For this reason, we go into the backcountry—the school of self-denial—where we voluntarily take on the hardships of traversing rugged and impossible terrain in order to purify the self of its egoist and comfort-driven excess. Saint Ignatius of Loyola, in his *Spiritual Exercises*, describes this as foundational:

> By the term "Spiritual Exercises" is meant every method of examination of conscience, of meditation, of contemplation, of vocal and mental prayer, and of other spiritual activities that will be mentioned later. For just as taking a walk, journeying on foot, and running are bodily exercises, so we call Spiritual Exercises every way of preparing and disposing the soul to rid itself of all inordinate

attachments, and, after their removal, of seeking and finding the will of God in the disposition of our life for the
salvation of our soul.[3]

But for Saint Ignatius and the entire tradition, self-denial
is a means and not the end. Accordingly, we can view
mountain climbing, itself a spiritual exercise, as the training ground for a deeper work. Returning to the first principle and foundation of human life, Saint Ignatius writes:
"Man is created to praise, reverence, and serve God, and
by this means to save his soul."[4] When we set out on the
trail, and do so with the intention of making it a spiritual
exercise, we must shift our intention from ourselves to
God. We offer our climbs in praise of him, that we might
reverence and serve him more deeply. This is a supernatural path, known only in Christ—and it is the one that leads
ultimately to being conquered by the love of God.

Setting aside the modern presuppositions of Mallory's
insight, the phrase "because it's there" is a powerful testimony to the Christian metaphysics of creation. This theme,
so central to our trail letters, means that creation, by its
very being, speaks of the Creator God—whom we know
as Father through the Incarnate Son. Why do we climb?
Because the interplay of deep immersion in the created
realm matched by its transcendent heights impresses upon
us a sense of our creatureliness. It signals a retreat from our
modern, technocratic society and its unquenchable desire for
the conquest and consumption of all. The wild, precarious,
and uninhabitable locales of the high places awaken us again
to the realness of things and, thereby, the realness of God.

[3] Ignatius of Loyola, *Spiritual Exercises*, trans. Louis Puhl, S.J. (Westminster,
Md.: Newman Press, 1951), no. 1.
[4] Ibid., no. 23.

In a world created by the inestimable, infinite love of God, every creature possesses its own particular nature, goodness, and perfection. Through the *logos*, all things came to be with an inexpressible richness, diversity, and order. Our task is to "recognize the inner nature, the value, and the ordering of the whole of creation to the praise of God."[5] Praise, that most basic form of prayer, arises naturally out of the heart that interprets "because it's there" to mean "because He is love." In this way, we can affirm with Guardini: "We owe the world to God."[6] Within this striking awareness that the world has been given to us on loan, we come to understand that it has likewise been entrusted to us with its perfection. And this is the source of our praise.

One evening, high up above the town of Telluride, I experienced this. The aspens were quietly blowing in the wind, while a chorus of birds offered up their evensong. I realized in that moment that the vast expanse of creation, truly unthinkable before me, was doing two things at once: it was *being*, and, by being, it was praising. I then realized that man, as the summit of creation, was created within this symphony of praise. As Romano Guardini describes:

> This is not a fairy-tale approach to nature in which the sun and the moon, the trees, and so forth are personalized and given voices with which to sing the praise of God; it is an inspired poetic rendering of the idea that the sun and the moon and all created things are a mirror of God's glory because, as His creation, they reflect something of His nature. In so doing, they praise Him by their very

[5] *Catechism of the Catholic Church*, no. 337.
[6] R. Guardini as quoted in H.U. von Balthasar, *Romano Guardini: Reform from the Source*, trans. Albert K. Wimmer and D.C. Schindler (San Francisco: Ignatius Press, 2010), 18.

existence. They themselves know nothing of it, but man does; he can think himself into their silent song of praise; he can voice it on their behalf, offer it up to God and thus act as the spokesman of creation.[7]

Endowed with the gifts of reason and freedom, we have the task of knowing and choosing in love to enter into the task of co-responsibility with God for the perfection of creation. One is called to be, as Guardini said, "the spokesman of creation". It is then antithetical to our humanity to subjugate creation to conquest. Because if creation is absolute reception, then our freedom is at the service of its creator. Everything is given in love for the creature, but as an invitation to the communion of divine self-giving. Herein lies the Christian interpretation of Mallory's "because it's there".

At the beginning of his Letter to the Romans, Saint Paul offers a key synthesis of both the Christian metaphysics of creation as well as the necessity of conversion from our ungodly egocentrism to reverential praise. "Ever since the creation of the world his invisible nature, namely, his eternal power and deity, has been clearly perceived in the things that have been made. So they are without excuse ... because they exchanged the truth about God for a lie and worshiped and served the creature rather than the Creator" (Rom 1:20–25).

Because creation "is there", God can be clearly perceived. But why is it that we don't see him? Because, as Saint Augustine so powerfully formulated, the heart of man must decide between the loving praise of the City

---

[7]R. Guardini, *The Art of Praying: The Principles and Methods of Christian Prayer*, trans. Prince Leopold of Loewenstein-Wertheim (Manchester, NH: Sophia Institute Press, 1995), 58.

of God or the *libido dominandi* of the City of Man. And in a post-Christian world, where a practical atheism dominates and oppresses so much of our lives, the perception of God is eclipsed and the intelligibility of the act of praise totally undermined. And it is this spirit that afflicts not only the George Mallorys of the world but those of us in the Church as well. As the thoughtful and prophetic Frenchwoman Madeleine Delbrêl reflected, the loss of the sense of God in creation is a fundamental danger for the life of the Church and the world:

> In the new milieus it is the man-matter relation that ought most to occupy Christian attention. This relation has been forged in complete silence about God. By a strange act of submission, creation has taken the place of the creator. And since it happened in silence, we haven't been alerted to it. A fundamental danger has been noiselessly overtaking the Church: it is the danger of an age and a world in which God will no longer be denied or forced away, but simply excluded. He will be merely unthinkable. It is the danger of a world in which we will want to go and cry out his Name, but we will be unable to, because there will be no place for us to get a foothold.[8]

Madeleine wrote these words shortly after Hillary and Norgay summited Everest. How much more real have they become in our day, where the *ethos* of techno-nihilism is accelerating at an unimaginable pace. But like Madeleine, we return back to the basic truth of creation: that the God of love expresses himself in a knowable relation through Jesus Christ—he who has conquered the world. In Jesus, we recover the central *telos* of creation, that it is ordered,

---

[8] M. Delbrêl, *We, the Ordinary People of the Streets* (Grand Rapids: Eerdmans, 2000), 231.

not to conquest, but to sabbath rest and the contemplative repose of abiding love.

Making our last descent off the rolling hills of Sargents Mesa, I consulted my map and saw that we were approaching mile marker #300 of the Colorado Trail. Looking up, I saw the glorious sight of "trail magic"—those kindly souls appearing at random on the trail, this time making pancakes. I could hear subtle yelps from the band of Corgis, now knowing that the end of their seventy-mile share in our trek was coming to a close.

There was so much energized anticipation in those last miles that the thru-hikers started to run. But there were still several miles to go, and we were still wearing heavy packs. As the old man in the group, my adrenaline soon waned. Just as my tank emptied and I was about to collapse, our support car came around the corner, filled with friends, resupply, and a case of Coors. Waiting for the Corgis, we again assumed the casual walking pace of victory as we passed together at the finish line of Highway 119.

As ridiculous as the Derping Corgis had been, they had proven themselves through perseverance and were counted among our number as brothers-in-arms. We made our way north by car to the town of Crested Butte—the Rivendell of the American West. We feasted that evening like kings and shared in the joys that flow only from hard-fought endurance. It was a magical evening, an event of true communion among God and men, and it enfolded within that simple yet powerful assertion of the reality of creation. *Because it's there*. Or better put—*because He was there*.

21

AGERE SEQUITUR ESSE

The stillness of morning made me uncomfortable. But as my gaze moved from the steam of the coffee mug to a wildflower at my side, my restlessness subsided. Locals told me the flower was called an Elephant Head: bright and magenta, I saw how its top petal bulges and then tapers in the shape of trunk. It seemed to me, at least in that moment, to be the most magnificent of the over three thousand species of wildflowers that bloom each year in Colorado.

Crested Butte, my native homeland and the place of our rest day, is known as the wildflower capital of the world. Each summer it displays the unimaginable complexity of intelligent design and divine gratuity. Millions come to be and pass away, most of which are never to be seen by humans. It is, in the mind of a Christian, one of the most powerful testimonies of a God who loves beauty simply because it is beautiful—and creates it in a joyful squandering of love.

The hidden secret beneath Crested Butte's wildflowers is Mancos Shale. This soft stratum of the earth was a marine environment deposited around 90 million years ago, while the valley was filled by the North American Inland Sea. Sixty million years later, magma rose through the Earth's crust and began penetrating the native Mancos Shale. This created intense mineralization and the rise of laccoliths, peaks of unusual feature such as the Crested Butte. The terrain is fiercely beautiful, but the rainfall limited; which is strange for being a place of such compelling lushness. Were it not for the Mancos Shale, Crested Butte would be a high mountain desert. For this subtle and delicate stratum retains the water from the winter snow, releasing it ever so carefully so as to provide for the rich vegetation of its soil and create the fruitful cornucopia of wildflowers. All this for the Elephant Head at my side.

It's always been hard for human beings to slow down. The reasons for this are many, but the deepest one was described by Saint Augustine: "You made us for yourselves, and our hearts are restless until they rest in you."[1] The human heart is inherently restless, the deepest source of our constant activism. So long as I keep moving and doing, I will not have to face the restlessness of my heart. But when we attend to the heart, we see the cause of the restlessness—the human need to fulfill the desires of the heart. So begins the existential hunt for the perfect moment, a grasp at Paradise. But as soon as we taste it, it passes; and the heart feels again the ache of unfulfillment.

In addition to this are three cultural forces at play that are making it exponentially harder to slow down, quit the activity, and live from the heart. The first of these is the modern understanding of happiness as well-being. Most especially in affluent societies, the baseline presupposition of the good life consists in material comfort. This bourgeois conviction is epicurean in nature; we must pursue the maximal enjoyment of comfort, pleasures that only

[1] Augustine, *Confessions*, I.1.

wealth can afford. In reaction to this is a second force at play—Marxism. This ideological vision of human flourishing is not confined to the Soviet world of the past but is alive and well in our contemporary day. Marx, in explicitly denying the metaphysical notion of being, builds his project of material dialectics on the simple fact that man's dignity lies in what he does (and not in who he is). In this way, any of us who live an activistic life are anonymous Marxists. Lastly and most demonstrably, the technological paradigm has radically altered the human experience. As we have discussed in past letters, technology is itself morally neutral; but the technocratic, like the Marxist and bourgeois, is undermining the primacy of being.

Crested Butte is a place to which people come to escape from the frenetic madness of our activistic age. But it is interesting to note that the townsfolk are, for the most part, decidedly not Christian. Attempting to build a secular paradise is a neo-pagan project and always subject to ideological forces. What, then, does the Christian have to say for himself in a place such as this?

We begin with a penetrating axiom from the medieval world: *agere sequitur esse* (action follows being). The first thing the Christian must do to live in the midst of these forces is to assert within himself the primacy of being. What we do flows from what we are; and what we are is created. We must begin by the self-discovery of the uniqueness of our being, which we can only understand through knowledge of our creator. The primacy of being over action reorients my entire life on a new trajectory; instead of attempting self-actualization through what I do, I can discover it in the relational grounds of who I am. But as moderns we look to ourselves and deny this relational ground a priori. Furthermore, we equate "the intensity of desire with the achievement of success".[2] This is a problematic assumption that leads only to deeper *angst*. I am made for the communion of love, and that love is already woven into my very being. Any action in accord with this primordial love must flow from it. All action follows being.

How, then, do we go about reaffirming the primacy of being over action? The Greeks called it *theoria*, or leisure. Translated into Latin as *contemplatio*, the ancient notion of leisure is the highest human act and the one in which we find our deepest and most profound happiness. Leisure is the contemplative beholding of reality, the human act most akin to human *being*. As Josef Pieper beautifully describes: "The ultimate fulfillment, the absolutely meaningful activity, the most perfect expression of being alive, the deepest satisfaction, and the fullest achievement of human existence must needs happen in an instance of beholding, namely in the contemplative awareness of the world's ultimate and intrinsic foundations."[3]

In the quiet attention of the Elephant Head wildflower at my side, my heart opens to reality and recalls to me that things are beautiful simply because they are; and that I am beautiful simply because I am. These are the concrete touchpoints to the eternally beautiful God, the source and fountain of all being. This is what Romano Guardini calls us to, precisely in the post-Christian milieu of a neo-pagan Crested Butte.

As Christianity ceases to appear self-evident, the feeling that the world is something "given" and secure lessens. The man who decides to be a Christian will have opened

---

[2] R. Guardini, *The Life of Faith*, trans. John Chapin (Westminster: Newman Press, 1961), 41.

[3] J. Pieper, *Only the Lover Sings: Art and Contemplation*, trans. Lothar Krauth (San Francisco: Ignatius Press, 1990), 22.

to him the true nature of things ... he will not make of
that feeling a philosophy of defiant affirmation of existence; he will, rather, perceive that God is true Being, and
that "the form of the world passes away."[4]

A life of leisure opens us up to the nature of things. It is
the receptive posture of a loving trust in truth, goodness,
and beauty—but not for the sake of the purposes of man,
but because of the meaning of God. For too long Christians have sought to possess the world, albeit running contrary to the call of Christ. And leisure, that act by which
we contemplatively behold the being of things, is the path
to freeing us from the compulsive spirit of possession. As
Pieper concludes, "The happy life does not mean loving
what we possess but possessing what we love."[5] Only by
possessing the beloved, in an act of beholding God, can we
truly love all things.

It is beautiful to think of Jesus as the man of perfect leisure and contemplation. To be with him would have been
astonishing: here he is, recollected in himself, so entirely
self-composed, never anxious, never insecure—all his
actions flowing perfectly from his being. His gaze would
have penetrated to the depths of our hearts; his masculine
bearing offering the safe confidence of love's most intimate glance. Jesus looks at us and sees the Father, just as
he did the wildflower, the sparrow, and the mountain. In
his gaze, we discover the nature of God and the source
of his life. For God is the perfect unity of being and act,
the very place we are made to recline (cf. Ps 23). Left to

[4] R. Guardini, *The Faith and Modern Man*, trans. Charlotte E. Forsyth (New York: Pantheon Books, 1952), 138.

[5] J. Pieper, *Happiness and Contemplation*, trans. Richard and Clara Winston (South Bend: St. Augustine's Press, 1998), 63.

ourselves, we can never reconcile our action to our being. But in the posture of contemplative repose, our hearts rest in He who unites all action in the being of love. When Jesus invites us into the backcountry to "come away ..., and rest a while" (Mk 6:31), he is recalling all of creation to sabbath rest in him.

♦ ♦ ♦

We clung desperately to the hours of that rest day. Tomorrow would bring the final chapter and most arduous of challenges—entry into the San Juan Mountains, a perilous passage. We had spent that day in the presence of friends and bid farewell to our beloved Corgis.

Then the new group arrived, the most rag-tag of them all. Being a random assortment of priests and young guys, I had hesitations as to whether this group would cohere. We were heading out into a very remote area—this time without an evacuation plan.

That evening the new recruits assembled for our usual bag inspection. By now, we were merciless with over-packing. I gave my usual speech, hoping to instill excitement and apprehension over what we were about to undertake. Then my lieutenants, Luke, Cody, and Casey, took them all to task over their gear preparations. Soon it became evident that this group had a different feel, that they weren't going to do what we asked of them. It was then that they became known as the "Libertarians". As we would soon find out, they would be the most challenging and dangerous group we brought on the Colorado Trail.

I returned to that chair by the Elephant Head—this time with a whiskey. In the company of friends, we spent those final hours of our rest day *just being*. I will never forget how the leisure of that day changed my life, marked as one of the happiest I will ever know. I learned again "the one thing ... needful" (Lk 10:42)—to simply be with Jesus in all things. A quiet prayer rose from my heart that night: Lord, make my heart like the Manchos Shale; a hidden, priestly stratum containing the love of God that, in time, would bear the fruit of spiritual wildflowers in souls.

22

THE PROBLEM WITH FREEDOM

With great reluctance, we climbed out of the car and bid farewell to our friends in Crested Butte. It was the hardest goodbye on the trip. Looking westward, I saw the harsh, barren landscape of the Cochetopa Hills present itself again with stark and sobering beauty. How vastly different this was from the lush valley of the Crested Butte, only seventy miles to the north.

Before we even stepped on the trail, we encountered our first hiker. His countenance was battle worn and utterly defeated. He relayed to us a message of foreboding: his eastbound passage through the San Juans had been marked by twenty straight days of hail—and he was calling it. His words sent a chill down the group's spine. Our resupply crew offered him a ride to the local town of Gunnison, and we bid him farewell.

Now stepping onto the trail, things started to disintegrate. The Libertarians began their tacit declaration of independence, unwilling to work with our tried-and-tested team dynamics. They were not going to listen, and this was going to cause problems. Not long after this, the group disseminated and lost track of each other.

Then things got worse. I knew that today would be our driest day on the trail, but had no idea how desperate it would be. After a long morning march through the arid, ranching valley below Cochetopa Dome, we at last arrived at our only potential water source of the day. And it was horrific. It wasn't a water source, but a depository of cow dung with a drizzle of liquidity. We would have gladly drank from the cow trough on Sargents Mesa a hundred times over. But there was no choice—risk the drink now or collapse from dehydration later.

Pressing on into the hills southwest of the valley, we saw once again our mountainous thoroughfare—San Luis Peak, standing in majesty far off in the distance. It was the pole star of our final chapter of the trail; once we had passed it, we would be into the San Juan Mountains and begin our greatest and final adventure. But adventure was already upon us, as the storm clouds off San Luis took dead aim. With the group in diaspora, the storm broke open in the treeless valley. It brought again the shocking sight of proximate lightning and the harrowing echo of its accompanying thunder. Had we been together, we could have reached safety; but instead, chaos ensued, as we were helpless, scattered across the valley floor.

Freedom is a problem. We felt it that day in the Cochetopa Valley, just as any who has ventured to love knows the risk of rejection. Of all God's creatures, man is uniquely endowed with the capacity for free will, to elect and determine his course and destiny. The freedom of man flows from the soul, which, being rational, is elevated to a level incomparable to the plants and animals around him. Though freedom is a gift, one allowing the possibility of true love, it is likewise the instrument of the heart's torture.

I first thought of freedom as a problem when I read Dostoevsky's account of the "Grand Inquisitor". Told by Ivan Karamazov, the story elucidates how Jesus intensifies the problem of freedom when he comes to make man free.

In response, the Church has attempted to "alleviate" man's freedom by creating a system of servile obedience. As the Grand Inquisitor says to Christ: "Nothing has ever been more insufferable for man and for human society than freedom!... Instead of taking over men's freedom, you increased it still more for them!... There is nothing more seductive for man than the freedom of his conscience, but there is nothing more tormenting either."[1]

According to Ivan, we would rather Christianity remove our freedom and "save us from ourselves" than demand that we convert to Christ and become free. As exaggerated as this may sound, our contemporary moralistic presentations of the faith show how seductive this still is. In the end, Ivan's idea of the Catholic Church is a falsified one, a radical degeneration of the Christian project. It is always through the medium of the Church that Jesus, the mediator to God, makes us free.

We must begin again by acknowledging freedom as a problem. The best way to do that is to enter into a lived and concretely experienced form of communion, such as the marital, priestly, or religious common life. Like our desperate band on the Colorado Trail, the interpersonal drama of finite freedoms plays out on the stage of human life. Massimo Camisasca reflects on this, but takes it in a direction different from that of the Inquisitor:

> If we do not see our brother as an obstacle, we cannot love him. Unless we are altogether spiritualistic or superficial, we cannot help noticing, at certain moments of our life, the weight of the other who is placed at our side ... the weight of his perceptions, background, and different personal temperament. These differences can show up even in someone whom we otherwise consider to be extraordinarily close. It

[1] F. Dostoevsky, *The Brothers Karamazov*, trans. Richard Pevear and Larissa Volokhonsky (New York: Everyman's Library, 1992), 252–54.

is at this point that we discover the meaning of the sacramental presence of the other; we understand that his otherness or diversity is a sign of a Presence that transcends the
other and makes him a sign of something more.[2]

Now the contrast is drawn to the fore: the Grand Inquisitor wants to sublimate freedom in order to resolve the
problem, while the true logic of Christian life is a divine
method of transcending the problem. When I encounter
the other as opposite to me, I see the need for something categorically greater. The struggle itself conveys a
sacramental presence—that is, a sign pointing to the "all
the more real" Presence that is God. In other words, the
arena of finite freedoms points us to the source. The only
way this battle of freedoms makes sense is if it is interpreted as participation in the good and, by way of it,
participation in God's freedom. True, my freedom is self-
determining; but I am not the interpreter or the deepest
agency of my freedom. As Guardini concludes: "Man's
freedom is a created freedom and it therefore develops
essentially before God and in subordination to Him—all
the more so since God is not only creator of being but
also ground of truth and source of good."[3]

The truth of freedom lies, not in doing whatever I
want, but in conforming myself to reality. The good lies
outside of me, and the truth of my being is found only in
God, the author of my life. This is the real source of my
self-determination. Now instead of viewing Christianity
as an inherent denial of freedom, we view it as something
I grow into—an educative project. For this reason, Giussani will say that when "reality awakens responsibility",

[2] M. Camisasca, "Priestly Fraternities: Living the Sacrament of the Other",
in *Communio* 29 (Summer 2002): 255.

[3] R. Guardini, *Freedom, Grace, and Destiny: Three Chapters in the Interpretation
of Existence*, trans. John Murray, S.J. (New York: Pantheon Books, 1961), 81.

freedom becomes "the goal of education".[4] This is the essence of true Christian education: entry into Christ is the path to true human freedom. It is the heart of conversion and, in the afterlife, the essence of Purgatory. As Dante describes, the reason to climb the Mount of Purgatory is *"libertà va cercando"* (to go in search of freedom).[5] All this brings to fulfillment the promise of Christ: "If you continue in my word, you are truly my disciples, and you will know the truth, and the truth will make you free" (Jn 8:32).

How then do we go about acquiring true freedom in this life? We need a readiness to change as a fundamental precondition. It is this attitude alone that grounds the project of freedom and makes it a reality. This notion is championed by Dietrich von Hildebrand, who sees in it the absolute prerequisite of Christian existence. "All true Christian life, therefore, must begin with a deep yearning to become a new man in Christ, and an inner readiness to 'put off the old man'—a readiness to become something fundamentally different."[6]

If we desire to become another man, one different from the one we presently are, then the possibility of true freedom is before us. Readiness implies a desire for change and a new beginning. But only when I am convinced that the good is outside of me can it become a transformative agent. God created goodness in itself; and the purpose of human freedom is to conform to it. The more I choose the good, the more I am free. How different this is from the blind errancy of postmodern self-creation. From this vantage point, we realize Christian perfection

---

[4] L. Giussani, *The Risk of Education*, trans. Rosanna M. Giammanco (New York: Crossroad, 2001), 135–36.

[5] Dante, *Purgatorio*, Canto 1:70.

[6] D. von Hildebrand, *Transformation in Christ: On Christian Attitude* (San Francisco: Ignatius Press, 2001), 3.

is something entirely different from the confined and frustrated experience of moralism. Human perfection before God consists in readiness, what von Balthasar calls existential "pliancy".[7] In being made pliable through the open readiness of my will, the problem of my freedom finds its solution in Christ. As von Balthasar concludes: "The only act by which a human being can correspond to the God who reveals himself is the act of unlimited readiness. It is the unity of faith, hope, and love."[8]

It is said that Alexander the Great led his army over 11,000 miles on foot throughout their conquest of the known world. At one point, when a problem arose, he marched them back 180 miles in three days.[9] Any Libertarian on the trail that day would have likened his experience to being in the army of Alexander. It was the problem of freedom, presenting itself in new historical circumstances.

Enduring those final hours of the storm, but now within the cover of a forest, our group regained its integrity. Passing over a final ridgeline, we descended and found ourselves in a geological disparity—the harsh landscape of the day transfigured into the verdant dell of the Cochetopa Creek. Camping on the soft grass by the rolling edge of the creek felt like a dream; and we drank deeply as if we had never tasted water before. The giftedness of that place occasioned a transformation: the cooperative problem of freedom was now resolving into a collective readiness to change.

[7] H. U. von Balthasar, *The Glory of the Lord: A Theological Aesthetics*, vol. 1, *Seeing the Form*, trans. Erasmo Leiva-Merikakis (San Francisco: Ignatius Press, 1982), 221.

[8] H. U. von Balthasar, "Vocation", in *Communio* 37 (Spring 2010): 116.

[9] W. Carroll, *A History of Christendom*, vol. 1: *The Founding of Christendom* (Front Royal: Christendom Press, 1985), 197–202.

23

DON'T FORGET YOUR BISCUITS

"Yahweh is a tricky Yahweh", my old confessor used to say. In just those moments when we take ourselves too seriously, God seems to have the greatest laugh. And this held true that very morning, as we approached a seemingly impossible creek crossing. The scene was truly comical: there we were, thru-hikers and libertarians, arm-in-arm, barefoot and imbalanced, staged across the rapids. All psychological issues were dissolved in the strangeness of the physical moment. Were one to fall, all would take a long swim downstream— and it was only six o'clock in the morning.

We did indeed cross, breathed a sigh of relief, and relaced our shoes. Setting out again on dry land, we began our steady climb into the basin below San Luis Peak. Only fifteen miles and a few thousand feet of elevation, the day was to be a welcomed deceleration from the intensity of the one prior. Passing the trailhead of Eddiesville (an abandoned mining outpost), we set into our fifth wilderness area, known as La Garita.

This "law of divine comedy" reminded me of an experience years ago on Little Bear Peak. Considered by many to be the most challenging fourteener in the state, Little Bear is a granite fortress, stationed far south of the Sangre de Cristo Range. Its infamy lies in a passageway known as the "hourglass", the most accessible route into the citadel.

The rock within the hourglass is pulverulent and danger-ously loose. If it should fall, the passage of the hourglass becomes a life-size bowling alley—one in which you have the ill-fortune of being the pin.

My trusted climbing partner, Mike, and I set out to climb Little Bear in the spring of 2013. Our plan was to do it early in the season and climb it in the snow (which substantially lessens the risk of rockfall). At the eleventh hour, Mike asked if his friend could join us, to which I agreed. Now Mike is a faithful Catholic and one with whom I had shared many a fourteener Mass. But his friend was, I came to find out, an agnostic Jew. You can imagine the perplexed look on his face when I attempted to explain what I was going to do at the summit.

We packed into Lake Como the night before and pitched camp in the snow just below treeline. For what-ever reason, I took the hosts from my Mass kit and placed them in the bear bag, hung a short distance from camp. In order to have the best possible snow conditions, we set out that next morning at 2:30 a.m., made our long traverse to the base of the climb, and started up the hourglass with crampons and ice axe. Despite the frigid cold of that sum-mit sunrise, I was elated as I set up for Mass on the most challenging of Colorado's high peaks. Then I reached into my kit and was struck with horror—I had left the hosts in the bear bag at camp. I sat there, devastated and inter-nally raging. It was then that my agnostic Jewish climbing partner put his arm around me and said with the utmost sincerity and tender concern: "Father, I'm really sorry you forgot your biscuits."

I will always laugh at the strangeness of the comment and how it lifted me out of my spiral of self-pity. But reflecting more deeply, to think that postmodern man would look at the Eucharist as "biscuits" was really quite instructive. It occasioned me, once again, the opportunity to think more profoundly over the nature of our Catholic worldview—and just how foreign it is to our contemporaries. For then again, how do we get from an event in Palestine two thousand years ago to this bread at the top of a mountain? This would require a few theological stepping stones.

First, the foundation of the Christian worldview is revelation. God has disclosed himself, truly revealed himself, by an act of his own initiative and loving free will. Christians call this the "economy of salvation", or the plan in which God comes to man in order to draw him back into communion. For centuries, God spoke and worked through the Old Covenant with his chosen people, the Jews. "But when the time had fully come, God sent forth his Son ... so that we might receive adoption as sons" (Gal 4:4–5). The Incarnation of the God-Man, Jesus Christ, is the apex of God's self-revelation; he has not come just to reveal things about himself, but he is truly with us in human form. As Saint Paul writes: "He is the image of the invisible God, the first-born of all creation; for in him all things were created ... all things were created through him and for him" (Col 1:15–16).

Far from being a religious sage or model for good living, Jesus Christ is the total revelation of God. By total we mean absolute, definitive, and complete—and this is where the modern world takes offense. As Giussani remarks: "A religion may commit only one crime: to say 'I am the religion, the one and only way.' And this is precisely what Christianity claims."[1] To a culture that rejects any abso-

---

[1] L. Giussani, *At the Origin of the Christian Claim*, trans. Viviane Hewitt (Montreal: McGill-Queen's University Press, 1998), 28.

lute and universal claims, the idea of Christianity is utterly insulting. The modern then attempts to relativize Christian faith, counting Jesus as one religious figure among many, and his path, one of many up the same mountain. But by doing so, we annihilate the integrity of revelation and deny the irreputable uniqueness of Christ. And as we have seen, when revelation is disregarded, the object of religion becomes "Nature".

In addition to revelation, the second stepping stone into the Christian worldview is the notion of sacramentality. Oftentimes we think of sacraments as commodities, things that we receive on our journey through Catholic life. But sacramentality is far more—it is the structure and inner logic of God's revelation. Firstly, Jesus Christ is the sacrament of God. It is in him that we come to know the Father; in and through his words and actions that God is truly revealed. Sacramentality is foremost a Christological reality, something manifest when God assumed a human nature and entered into creation. Then, we can speak of a second, ecclesiological mode—namely, that the Church is the sacrament of Christ. Far from being a mere sociological aggregate, the Church is the mystery of Christ extended throughout history. Speaking about Christ, Saint Paul tells us that just as " 'the first man Adam became a living soul'; the last Adam became a life-giving spirit" (1 Cor 15:45). It is now the pneumatic body of Christ that we receive; his true and real presence extended throughout all times and places.

One last stone must then be placed. If the foundation of the Christian worldview is revelation, and the mode of that revelation is sacramentality, then the heart of sacramentality is the Eucharist. Described by the Church as the source and summit of the faith, the Eucharist is the Real Presence of Jesus Christ, veiled under the accidents of bread and wine. Everything hinges on those beautiful words of institution: "Take, eat; this is my body" (Mt 26:26). As von Balthasar poetically writes: "In this garment of bread and wine he desires to dwell among us with his bodily presence, sharing in men's joys and sorrows."[2] Jesus creates the Eucharist as the *source* in order to communicate the fullness of his sacrificial and redeeming love on the Cross. He likewise established it as the *summit*, because within it we glimpse the heights of Trinitarian love. From all eternity, the Son receives the total gift of self from the Father, and the exchange of that gift is given to us in the Eucharist.

There were many forms of sacrifice in the Old Covenant. But there was one of particular significance, offered in the Temple when a person's life had been redeemed or delivered from a great danger. This was called the *todah* sacrifice—the sacrifice of thanksgiving (cf. Lev 7:13–15). The Hebrew word *todah* does mean thanksgiving, but it also means "praise", and even "confession". As the centuries passed and an eschatological vision deepened, the Jews came to see that in the end, only one sacrifice would remain—the *todah*. When Jesus takes bread into his hands, he establishes his Eucharistic love of the Father as the eternal *todah*. And in the hours that followed, he stood as the priest and victim on the Cross, shedding his blood for the forgiveness of sins (cf. Heb 9:22). This is the summit of faith, completed on the mountain of Calvary. Through the re-presentation of Christ's Eucharistic offering, the inner man is awakened and his heart rises to God. An ancient phrase for the Eucharist is the "sacrifice of praise"—which, as Ratzinger describes, is the source of our ascent to God.

[2] H. U. von Balthasar, *Heart of the World*, trans. Erasmo S. Leiva (San Francisco: Ignatius Press, 1979), 128.

"Through the praise of God man ascends to God. Praise itself is a movement, a path; it is more than understanding, knowing, and doing—it is an 'ascent', a way of reaching him who dwells amid the praises of the angels."[3] To my mind, there is no more fitting and beautiful place for the eternal *todah* sacrifice of the Son than on the physical summits of creation's heights.

We had climbed all day to the base of San Luis Peak. Our treeline campsite, just below 12,000 feet, was the highest we would have on the entire Colorado Trail. From that vantage point, we quieted and steadied our hearts for the central act of the day—the Holy Sacrifice of the Mass. Jesus was to become truly present in a most remote locale, in order to commune with a few men and draw them into the depths of his eternal praise and gratitude of the Father. In other words, I was very happy to have my biscuits.

As glorious as a mountain Mass can be, it does not remove the human challenge of the backcountry. Many of the Libertarians were beaten down, and though the day was reprieved, tomorrow would be a monster—a hard-fought twenty miles and 4,000 feet needed to get us to our next resupply. Even more, the thru-hikers, now galvanized machines, wanted to summit San Luis in the morning, adding more mileage and several thousand feet to the day's challenge. This would require another difficult conversation with the Libertarians. Fortunately, it was gracious and humble on both ends. The plan was as follows: half the group would make for the summit and complete the section, while the other half would head to the nearest

[3] J. Ratzinger, *Collected Works*, vol. 11, *Theology of the Liturgy: The Sacramental Foundation of Christian Existence*, trans. John Saward, Kenneth Baker, S.J., Henry Taylor, et al. (San Francisco: Ignatius Press, 2014), 434–35.

exit point, hitchhiking down through the town of Creede. The hope was that we would all meet and finish together at our resupply point, Spring Creek Pass.

For many years, I have wished to speak again with that agnostic Jewish man about the beauty of Christ's Eucharistic *todah*. It taught me about the chasmic difference between the revelatory-sacramental worldview of the Catholic and the secular-materialistic one inhabiting most people in the world. He also gave me a great gift, reminding me never to forget the centrality of the Eucharist in my worldview. And I will forever heed his advice: *Don't forget your biscuits.*

24

WORD AND SILENCE

We were moving fast, too fast. All I could see was the rock pile before me, illuminated by my head lamp. All I could hear was the belabored breathing of bodies moving into an anaerobic state. Other than that, there was only the silence and total darkness of a midnight ascent.

How did I get here? Alas, it was once again the conspiring of the thru-hikers—Luke, Casey, and Cody—and their insane idea from the night before. In addition to traversing the East San Juans to our resupply point on Spring Creek Pass, they wanted to summit the fourteener we had been looking at for the last week—San Luis Peak. And it was understandable: the peak was the great entryway to the San Juans, the Colorado's Trail's rite of passage into its most hidden and majestic lands. Twenty-seven million years ago, a volcano erupted in the place where we stood; now this consolidated pile of volcanic ash, carved as by an artisan over millennia, stood sentinel in the foreboding darkness of night.

As with most of the schemes plotted and hatched by my lieutenants, I conceded and found myself up the next morning at 1 a.m. We broke camp and made our way toward the saddle of the peak. We then turned northward and started up the mountain into the darkness. I knew San Luis to be the most remote and least climbed fourteener in the state. But I had no idea that for the first time in my life, I would stand on a mountaintop in perfect darkness.

At the summit, I experienced something of the total purity of creation. There we sat, now 2:30 in the morning, on the rooftop of the world, with no visible light except the stars. It was a place of utter silence, total stillness, and, despite being together, a place of true solitude. We had reached those unexplored pathways found only on the shores of the truly human. And it was peaceful, deeply peaceful: For "not as the world gives [peace] do I give [it]" (Jn 14:27). From that bird's-eye view of San Luis, the depths of man were being awakened by the living God.

"I will feed them with good pasture, and upon the mountain heights of Israel shall be their pasture" (Ezek 34:14). These strange and paradoxical words from the prophet Ezekiel describe the way in which God cares for the soul, as a shepherd his sheep. I am told by Scripture scholars that the mountain heights of Israel are one of the most uninhabitable regions of the world. But it is there, and precisely there, that God desires to pasture souls. With what is he feeding us? Like that night on San Luis, the heights call us back to the bedrock of human existence, to a pattern of living that we so quickly let slip away. This bedrock? The preconditions of contemplation that we call silence and solitude.

In our modern day, we often equate silence with the absence of noise and solitude the absence of people. But anyone who feels the draw of the backcountry knows it to be salutary. In an important way, silence and solitude need to be understood in relation to action; because within the ambit they provide, action is entirely and completely transformed. These twin sisters of the contemplative life offer a kind of metaphysical salve, without which we cannot be healed from our latent and de-humanizing activism. Within the space they create, the soul is re-habilitated and the primacy of *being* reasserted.

One of my favorite hikes in Italy was to the *Eremo* of Saint Francis, high up on Monte Subiaso above the town of Assisi. When you enter into this sanctuary, hidden within the woods below treeline, you see the sign, *Silenzio*. And beneath it, in Latin reads: *Ubi Deus, ibi pax* (where there is God, there is peace). All of us desire peace to reign in our hearts, itself a desire for God. But the secret to encountering God is silence. It is the foundation of all prayer, an existential *sine qua non*. Why is this the case? Because silence is no mere absence of activity, but is an action of God. Unlike solitude, which can be open or closed to God, "silence", writes von Balthasar, "has no possibility of being neutral to God ... it is dialogical whether it wants to be or not."[1]

We must once again grow accustomed to silence. We must learn to love it and fight with fierceness to keep it in our lives. Without it, our minds degenerate and reality is lost to us. As von Hildebrand describes: "Silence fulfills an important function in mental regeneration. It is only in the passivity of silence that the things which have deeply impressed us may resound and grow in our soul, and strike root in our being. Silence alone evokes that inward calm which is a prerequisite of recollection."[2]

In the spirit of silence, things awaken in our souls and begin to impress themselves upon us. We feel the meaningfulness of things, and they speak to us. And herein lies the essence of Christianity, different from the religions

[1] H. U. von Balthasar, *Science, Religion, and Christianity*, trans. Hilda Graef (London: Burns and Oates, 1958), 114.

[2] D. von Hildebrand, *Transformation in Christ: On Christian Attitude* (San Francisco: Ignatius Press, 2001), 142.

of the East: silence is not the end, but the beginning. From the primordial silence of his eternal and transcendent being, God speaks his Word. He speaks first the word of creation and then re-creates and fulfills that originating word in his Son, Jesus Christ. The Second Person of the Trinity *is* Word, who gives expression to the silence of the Father. But even the Father is not silence; for it is he who speaks a word of his Word in the depths of the Jordan and on the heights of Tabor: "This is my beloved Son"; "listen to him" (Mt 3:17, 17:5). God has truly spoken, and it is only in silence that his voice can be heard.

In addition to silence, the human soul needs solitude to flourish. Like its twin, solitude has been reduced to isolation, or the absence of other persons. But just as silence is the action of God the Word, solitude is the presence of God the Spirit. As Thomas Merton instructs us: "Go into the desert not to escape from other men but in order to find them in God."[3] For the Christian, solitude is never a movement away from others, but a gesture directed more profoundly toward others. Merton continues: "If you try to escape from this world merely by leaving the city and hiding yourself in solitude, you will only take the city with you into solitude."[4] Only in the discovery of God is solitude valorized and experienced as the way to communion.

I am always amazed by how many people I find moving solo throughout the backcountry of Colorado. Oftentimes it gives the impression that they are running from something and not *for* something greater. This is perhaps the reason why so few can open their hearts to God. It is indeed tragic if we set out into the high country for a

[3] T. Merton, *Seeds of Contemplation* (New York: New Directions, 1949), 42.
[4] Ibid., 57.

deeper experience of relationship and only find ourselves more deeply stuck in our isolation.

Solitude preconditions relationship with God, but it does not preclude the presence of others. Certainly, humans need experiences of physical solitude in order to live healthy lives; but for the Christian, interior solitude can be lived anywhere. As Romano Guardini reflects:

> Solitude stirs an awareness of his personality in a man caught up in a network of community relationships.... He experiences his uniqueness, which can be neither replaced nor displaced. And this has nothing to do with selfishness or self-aggrandizement. It is the foundation of man's being and worth—of the individual who, as a person, can never be a means to a further end and also of groups which, because they are human, can be formed only of persons. We have the obligation of penetrating into solitude, into the realm of "myself with myself alone," and it is often extremely difficult to do so, because it brings a man face to face with the forces and tensions of his interior life, with the exigent demands of conscience, and again with that particular void which renders association with the self so arduous and even unbearable and makes any exterior activity which distracts from it a welcome relief.[5]

As cheap as the word "unique" has become, many people live lives without ever knowing they are truly unrepeatable. It flows from the fact that I am created, originating from a mind of ungraspable, divine intelligence. In this sense, there is an existential obligation to solitude, that I cannot know myself apart from resting in the aloneness of my particular being. Not even the greatest of friends can know the totality

---

[5] R. Guardini, *Freedom, Grace, and Destiny: Three Chapters in the Interpretation of Existence*, trans. John Murray, S.J. (New York: Pantheon Books, 1961), 43.

of a human heart. Only in those solitary moments with the invisible God can we experience a communion that brings everlasting peace.

By now you know that Casey is a man who liked his solitude. Following our numinal experience of the midnight summit, we started down toward the saddle to meet the remaining Libertarians and make our way for the pass. Casey by this point had fallen well behind the group, almost out of sight. As we traversed a series of rolling valleys, we stopped at a small stream for water. It was still dark but the dawn was closing in. Suddenly, we heard a holler—or more of a prolonged yelp—echo in the valley behind us. There, a mile or so back, on the far side of the San Luis basin, was the solitary light of, undoubtedly, Casey. "Help", he cried "I need a ...", and the rest of the message was inaudible. At the same time, it was clear that one of the Libertarians was experiencing the onset of altitude sickness. It was necessary to march on to the nearest exit point; I continued with the group, sending Luke back to get Casey.

As we crested over San Luis Pass, dawn broke over the East San Juans. A herd of elk majestically rolled over the northern hillside, hastening for the valley below. Though we still had many miles and mountains between us and the day's end, the place provided access to West Willow Creek Trailhead, an exit point for those unable to continue.

At this point, Casey and Luke rejoined us, with grinning and bewildered faces. They then told the story of the ten-day needle. As you may recall, on day fourteen of the trail, our friend had to exit the Collegiate Peaks due to a series of indescribable blisters. Casey and Cody were lancing his blisters and preparing his feet for the hike out. For whatever reason, Casey took the needle used for lancing and placed it at his side—face up. Then, at some point, he managed to step on it, fully inserting it into his shoe. But he had no idea this had happened. And for the next ten days, that needle would slowly make its way farther and farther into his shoe. At last, on the side of San Luis, just after four o'clock in the morning, the needle had fully penetrated his shoe and began stabbing him. It was then, in a moment of desperation, that he yelled out, "Help, I need pliers!"

We continued westward, removing the needle and carefully leaving it face down. Passing through a maze of mountain valleys and passes, we at last stepped onto the Snow Mesa, a perfectly flat four-mile plateau situated just above 12,000 feet. Now the vista was remarkable—a comprehensive view of the West San Juans, steely beauties and our companions in the days to come. Stepping off the Mesa and onto the pass of Spring Creek, we were greeted by a resupply from my parents. We would spend the evening in the town of Lake City, resting with anticipation for what would be the most glorious stretch of the Colorado Trail.

As we emerged from the backcountry and saw the road, there they were—the Libertarians. They had made it to Creede and hitchhiked to the pass. Our campaign from Crested Butte was complete, and though not the easiest group, the story of our days together concluded in peace. Despite all the frustrations and challenges, the Libertarians taught an important lesson: that within the arena of human relationships, the only posture that leads to love is silent solitude before the living God.

25

THE MEASURE OF ALL THINGS

Bidding farewell to the town of Lake City, we took up the trail once again at Spring Creek Pass and headed due west into the heart of the San Juans. We were about to pass through its most beautiful terrain, called by locals "the Switzerland of America".

The trail climbed from the pass, putting us suddenly above treeline in a place of astonishing scenery. In every direction, we saw vast ranges, filled with unusual peaks, the progeny of great volcanoes. To the north glimmered Lake San Cristobal, formed only 760 years ago by a catastrophic mudslide. To the far west, we could see Carson Saddle, our day's journey and what would be the highest point on the Colorado Trail at 13,271 feet. After nineteen miles and 4,000 feet of climbing, we would settle into the aptly named Lost Trail Creek Basin for our evening camp.

But then everything changed. Cody approached and spoke with foreboding: "I have to ask you this question, but I'm afraid to ask it: Did you grab the group food from town?" Suddenly the premonition became reality—we had forgotten our food. Now, five miles into the trail, my parents (our resupply) were well on their way back to Denver. How the food was forgotten is a story for another time. How it was recovered was one of the most remarkable moments on the trail.

My mother is affectionately known as the world's greatest *putzer*. Being of German descent, she doesn't waste time—but given her highly sanguine and energetic personality, one wonders how focused her surges of daily activity may be. Though this style has, at times, driven me mad, I will never cease to be grateful after today. Had she left town with my Dad as planned, they would have been long gone and out of cell phone service, laded with four days of food for fifteen men in the back of their car. But miraculously, we found cell service and got a hold of her on the phone. There she was, putzing around Lake City, shopping here and bopping there. If she had not answered and been in town, our adventure on the Colorado Trail would have come to an immediate and tragic end.

The thru-hikers agreed to keep the new group moving, as we had to cover Carson Saddle before the afternoon storms. We divided Luke's pack between us, and he went in a dead sprint back five miles to meet my parents at the Pass. This was a tall order. To accomplish it, Luke would have to carry about fifty pounds of food up, making his day total well over a marathon. Shortly after this, we realized the burden we had put on Luke, and it was decided that I would wait for him. Cody and Casey pressed on with the group—and I kicked up my feet in the quiet of an aspen grove, waiting for lunch.

The problems of life, such as the misplacement of trail food, occasion deeper questions. Setting aside the emotional intensity of the moment, we have to find the quiet aspen groves of life and settle in. Problems in life fracture our systems and frustrate our plans; but they lead to the deeper questions of meaning. These are questions of *measure*, the "how to" for interpreting meaning. Humans have been doing this for millennia without even realizing it. Its first philosophical expression happened in the debate of two Greeks—Protagoras and Plato.

Protagoras, born in the fifth century, was a pre-Socratic philosopher and renowned rhetorician. He is most remembered for saying that "man himself is that measurement of all things."[1] Within unique speculative powers, man is able to interpret reality and thereby be called "the measure of all things". This worldview of Protagoras is anthropocentric—that things are meaningful according to how we measure them. This also informed his work as a sophist, "a wise-man for hire". For if man is the measure of all things, then perhaps the wisest among us (or in the case of the sophists, the most rhetorically compelling) can answer our questions on meaning.

Plato, born a generation later, would take up the line drawn by his great master, Socrates. In contrast to Protagoras, Plato affirms the opposite: "God is the measurement of all things."[2] Despite the limitations of what *theos* (god) may have been to Plato, the shift from Protagoras is revolutionary. The worldview moved from being anthropocentric to theocentric. God is the measure, which means man is himself measured. For Plato, we come to be measured through the knowledge of eternal truths, upon which he establishes the Greek educational ideal known as *paideia*. A word impossible to translate, *paideia* means culture, education, formation, or discipline. But most telling is its translation into Latin by Cicero—*humanitas*. Greek *paideia* is the cultivation of humanity or, better put, "nature humanized". Contrary to the sophist project of

---

[1] Protagoras quoted in W. Jaeger, *Humanism and Theology (Aquinas Lecture 7)* (Milwaukee: Marquette University Press, 1943), 51.

[2] Plato quoted in ibid., 53.

man as the measure, this platonic vision of education seeks to conform the person to reality—a reality established as meaningful and measured alone by God. In the end, Protagorean thought only leads to skepticism, a declaration of cultural bankruptcy.[3] What Plato provided for the world was the method for authentic human flourishing, what history would call *humanism*. We must first put man back in the world of being and, only then, seek to measure things through knowledge. Or, as von Balthasar put it: "The question of being includes the search for a light that sheds light on the meaning of man."[4] We find the meaning of ourselves only by understanding the measure of God.

As Christopher Dawson notes, "*paideia* was a humanism in search for a theology."[5] It found it in Christian revelation. The confluence of Greek metaphysical thought and Jewish salvation history was timed perfectly for the greatest event in history—the Incarnation of the God-man, Jesus Christ. When Saint John tells us "the Word became flesh" (Jn 1:14), we see the fulfillment of Greek *paideia* within the metanarrative of God's saving work. We also see the birth of theology, which, contrary to modern preconceptions, is a distinctively Christian act. Theology is the union of "word" (*logos*) and "flesh" (*history*) in the person of Jesus Christ. If his is the perfect humanity, then being educated in him is the perfect humanism. Jesus Christ, as God and man, is the measure of all things—the fulfillment of Plato and, ironically, even of Protagoras.

For centuries, Christians received this beautiful patrimony. It was the center upon which their worldview was

[3] Cf. ibid., 51.

[4] H. U. von Balthasar, *Epilogue*, trans. Edward T. Oakes (San Francisco: Ignatius Press, 2005), 22.

[5] C. Dawson, *The Crisis of Western Education* (Washington, D.C.: CUA Press, 2010), 7.

shaped. The Christian faith gave birth to monasteries and universities, harbingers of the true *paideia*. But with the advent of modernity, this began to collapse. The Renaissance of the sixteenth century sought to re-found an anthropocentric worldview and thereby re-enshrine man as the measure of all things. For the last five centuries, our worldview has been largely shaped by philosophical revolution: philosophy supplanted by science and now science subordinated to technology.[6] Modern scientific man believed his reason to be the measure of reality and, through it, worshipped at the altar of his own progress. Now, postmodern technological man seeks to immortalize his freedom as the ultimate, totalizing measure of reality. Once again, we have arrived at the worldview of self-creation, headed for the same cliff of relativism proposed by the sophists.

If our cultural salvation lies in a Christocentric worldview, how do we once again allow Jesus to measure our experience? In the words of Saint Paul: "That Christ may dwell in your hearts through faith; that you, being rooted and grounded in love, may have power to comprehend with all the saints what is the breadth and length and height and depth" (Eph 3:17–18). Breadth and length, height and depth—the measure of meaning in everything—is in Christ alone. But in the presence of Christ, man is not measuring, but *being* measured, first and foremost as a creature. This is why we immerse ourselves in creation; and to the extent that we do so in light of the Creator, creation affords us a sense of the measure.

Man is unique among animals; he desires to go beyond himself from without and discover himself from within. This could be described as transcendence and immanence—the

---

[6] Cf. von Balthasar, *Epilogue*, 23.

two poles by which we seek measure. And we see this in a natural way in the mountains: on the summits of high peaks, my heart reaches out to a seemingly infinite expanse, instilling in me a sense of transcendence. But then when I look down to behold the complex beauty of a Columbine flower, I am filled with the awe of immanence. And for the Christian, this is just the beginning. When we speak of God, we speak of total transcendence—that which is outside of creation, its mysterious and unknowable source. But then suddenly at the Incarnation, he enters into creation as a child in the womb, becoming totally immanent. This concrete event redefines man's experience of divine transcendence and immanence, revealing the mysterious inner logic of creation itself. Jesus Christ, the union of divinity and humanity, of transcendence and immanence, is now the only key and true measure. This is humanism par excellence, the pure *paideia* of faith. As Giussani eloquently summarizes: "Another has become our measure. Nothing is more humanly desirable for our nature; the very life of our nature is love, the affirmation of Another as the self's meaning."[7]

Minutes felt like hours as I waited in the aspen grove for Luke. We had sent the group deeper into the backcountry, on the promise that food would come. At last, my trusted lieutenant appeared over the horizon, laden with food and clearly energized by the challenge.

We made haste for the Carson Saddle. Among rolling hilltops, our mountain vistas expanded, as if transcending into the infinite. Upon the towering heights of the San Juan Mountains, one cannot help but to lose all sense

[7] L. Giussani, *At the Origin of the Christian Claim*, trans. Viviane Hewitt (Montreal: McGill-Queen's University Press, 1998), 102.

of measure. How fitting that the first Spanish explorers named them the *San Juans*—the mountains of Saint John. Of all the Evangelists, Saint John is known for soaring to contemplative heights, designated under the sign of the eagle (cf. Ezek 1:10). Johannine mysticism, a spiritual life rooted in the measure of Christ, is the only response to the rocky magnitude of southwestern Colorado.

We saw, far off in the distance, twelve black dots steadily making their way to the Coney Summit. We quickened our pace to catch them and arrived together at the rooftop of the Colorado Trail. There we enjoyed our most grateful lunch, attempting to measure the beauty and complexity of a truly epic day. Once again, we rediscovered the secret of the Christian: when you renounce yourself as the measure and take up that of Christ, you come to see the meaning of all things—that the measure of the Son is the immeasurable love of the Father.

26

DEUS ABSCONDITUS HAIC

The morning light had yet to penetrate the valley below, creating a kind of chiaroscuro upon the rolling terrain of the Lost Trail Valley. We embraced the chill of those first hours in the shade, knowing that once we reached our first pass, we would be decimated by the alpine sun.

If I were given only one segment of the Colorado Trail for the rest of my life, I would choose Segment 24—our present stretch between the towns of Lake City and Silverton. Here we found ourselves in one of the most remote locales in the country, on a trail as physically demanding as it is personally rewarding. We had been hiking for nearly a month but were still unprepared for the beauty we now encountered. Whatever happened during the Laramide Orogeny eighty million years ago, it created something unlike anything else. We were wounded by its beauty.

But we had twenty miles and 4,600 feet of elevation to climb before we could sit and take in our surroundings. Today was the great test that would make or break our most recent crew, "the Sulfites". Like most every group, they were named by the hallmark trait of their most ridiculous characters; and by the end of today, there were a few hikers that were so dehydrated that their faces were literally covered in salt.

In continuity with the days prior, our twelve-hour march was entirely above treeline. This meant a perpetual and expansive view of indescribable terrain. First, we passed westward, traversing the northern giants known as Handies, Redcloud, and Sunshine Peaks—all standing tall above 14,000 feet. We then turned south, moving into valleys and over passes of unspeakable breadth. The repose of lunch was cut short due to the aggressive advance of a thunderstorm. We made haste over Stony Pass before turning south and westward onto the everlasting hills of Cataract Ridge. But it was only then that we would glimpse the heart of the San Juans—the Needles, Vestals, and at their center, the Trinity Peaks. Here was the center of the mystery of the San Juans, a sight that lifted our souls out of the agony of the trail with the renewed vigor that only beauty can provide.

During my years living in Italy, I fell in love with road biking. The Italian sense for the *bella figura* applies as much to mountain roads as it does to stilettos and cappuccinos. The dream was to ride the Amalfi Coast, that narrow stretch of rocky terrain that juts out below the Bay of Naples and cuts back inland to the city of Salerno. Riding it one Sunday morning left me with two conclusions: this was certainly the most beautiful road ever created—and undeniably the most dangerous. I braced around every corner as Ducatis cut into my lane at 120 kilometers per hour. One mistake from them, and I was nothing more than pasta on the road.

At the end of the ride, I walked through the town of Amalfi and made for the cathedral. It was here, above the tomb of Saint Andrew, that I saw a side chapel for the Blessed Sacrament. And I was struck by what was written above: *Deus absconditus haic* (God is hidden here). There he was, a hidden mystery in the tabernacle, the dwelling place of the true presence of Jesus Christ.

Now mystery is not the first word that comes to mind when we think of Christianity. But as Matthias Scheeben observed, "Christianity entered the world as a religion replete with mysteries."[1] The Christian faith is wholly and completely mysterious; for it is *the* mystery of the supernatural presence of God in the world. But this mystery is not pure esotericism, a kind of non-rational mystification of things. It is the heights in which human reason seeks to climb, but one that cannot arrive on its own. As Giussani explains:

> Imagine that reason were a good mountain climber who scaled the highest summit on the globe and, once at the top, realized that the peak which he had just climbed was merely a small foothill leading to an enormous mountain whose beginning or end could not be seen. The summit of reason's conquest is the perception of an unknown unreachable presence, to which all human movement is destined, because it depends upon it. It is the idea of *mystery*.[2]

God is, above all, the mystery of faith. But he is knowable in and through his two books—creation and Scripture. The Fathers reflect on creation as a book that speaks mysteriously of God, which implies that creation is itself a mystery. This is revolutionary, especially in a rationalistic age seeking to conquer nature. Creation is a mystery. Whether biking the Amalfi Coast or climbing in the San Juans, it

---

[1] M. Scheeben, *The Mysteries of Christianity*, trans. Cyril Vollert, S.J. (New York: Crossroad, 2008), 3.

[2] L. Giussani, *The Religious Sense*, trans. John Zucchi (Montreal: McGill-Queen's University Press, 1998), 117.

harkens to us as mystery and calls us back to the originating mystery of God. As Giussani concludes: "Everything is born from the Mystery, nothing makes itself."[3]

Returning to the side chapel in Amalfi, we can probe more deeply into the distinctive nature of Christian mystery. Above all, mystery is a presence. Rooted in the event by which God became man, mystery is constituted as personal and relational, ultimately ordered to love. Being grounded wholly in the Incarnation, it is extended throughout all of history in the Church. But far from being a mausoleum of Christian artifacts, the Church is the living presence of Christ. It is the place where God lives in the world, itself a mystery. As we have said above, the Church is a sacramental mystery—and, at her core, Eucharistic. As Henri de Lubac wrote: "If the Church is thus the fullness of Christ, Christ in his Eucharist is truly the heart of the Church."[4] They live inexplicably from one another, meaning that together they reflect their essence—the Eucharistic gratitude of the Son.

Two things I often hear on the lips of secular companions in the mountains, both of which are important and fundamentally good: awe for the mystery of creation, and the phrase "I'm just grateful." As we saw above, these are both curious for the Christian, whose vision of mystery is intimately connected to gratitude. But when these two ideas, mystery and gratitude, are separated and secularized, they are emptied of their content. An example of this is given by a secular outdoorsman I recently read:

[3] L. Giussani, S. Alberto, and J. Prades, *Generating Traces in the History of the World: New Traces in the Christian Experience*, trans. Patrick Stevenson (Montreal: McGill-Queen's University Press, 2010), 56.

[4] H. de Lubac, *The Splendor of the Church*, trans. Michael Mason (San Francisco: Ignatius Press, 1986), 160.

If, as I had, you remove the answers provided by religious faith from the equation, you find that you enter the world from an incomprehensible realm of non-being—a void which no one understands in any meaningful way, only to be indoctrinated into a socially constructed idea of objective reality which takes place within the confines of an unfathomably vast and indifferent universe.[5]

Now I have no idea what that paragraph means—but I find it interesting. It strikes me as a thoughtful man, searching for meaning in a secular world. The architects of his thought are obvious: Friedrich Nietzsche, Martin Heidegger, and so forth. But the point is this: when mystery is jettisoned from its personalistic foundations in God, all it leaves us with is a kind of existential *angst* groping its way through the darkness of human life.

Secondly, it has become common mountain parlance to say the phrase, "I'm just grateful." This is a good start, but the sentence never gets completed. Gratitude for the mystery of creation implies a *who*, a someone to whom I offer thanks. I don't thank the espresso I had this morning, or the tree I passed on the trail. But I am made for gratitude, and it is the most fundamental response of anything created. As a professor of mine recently wrote: "I do not want to merely feel grateful. I want to be grateful, and being grateful, as opposed to merely feeling grateful, requires at least two conditions: that I recognize myself as one having received; and that I be recognized; and that I be recognized by the Other as grateful."[6]

Gratitude without otherness is empty, just as mystery without persons is bewildered. Yet this is the normative

[5] J. Hibbard, *The Art of Cycling: Philosophy, Meaning, and a Life on Two Wheels* (New York: Pegasus Books, 2023), 44.

[6] C. Thompson, *The Joyful Mystery: Field Notes Toward a Green Thomism*, (Steubenville: Emmaus Road Publishing, 2017), 148.

posture of the outdoor enthusiast. There are two options, as the Dostoevskian characters portray: the Elder Zosima, "for whom creation is one long invitation to thanksgiving", and Ivan Karamazov, who "refuses to accept it".[7] And as we see in the novel, this choice leads to one of two ends—gratitude or resentment. You cannot have both, but you will have one. In the end, it is not circumstances, but your freedom that will decide. The first path, gratitude, leads to communion and the dialogue of sacrificial love; the latter, resentment, to alienation and the monologue of victimhood. In the phrase "I'm just grateful", I hear the *cris de coeur* of postmodern man, seeking asylum from the inevitability of its cultural resentment. But it is only the eternal gratitude of Jesus Christ that truly sets us free.

If the mystery of creation is then "one long invitation to thanksgiving", Jesus Christ provides the key in his Eucharist. The Greek word for "thanksgiving", Eucharist is the true form that humans desire when they are "just grateful". It is not just the fullness of human life, but even the "source and summit" of faith.[8] And it is not merely a gesture; it is an event of tremendous consequences. On the night before he was to suffer for the sins of the world, Jesus instituted the Eucharist as the perennial form by which his sacrificial gift of self would be communicated. We are now at the heart of the mystery of redemption and the nexus point of the entire Catholic sacramental worldview. But sadly, the Eucharist can be detached from the event of Cross, and even the person of Jesus. We are tempted to "commodify" the Eucharist, in a consumeristic mentality, as a "thing" I get when I go to Mass. This leads to the inane and, at times, mind-numbing *disputatios*

[7] As cited in R. Guardini, *Freedom, Grace, and Destiny: Three Chapters in the Interpretation of Existence*, trans. John Murray, S.J. (New York: Pantheon Books, 1961), 119.

[8] *Catechism of the Catholic Church*, no. 1324.

around liturgical praxis and canonical liceity. To fall victim to this reduction is a sign that we have lost touch with the deeper reality of Christ—that the Eucharist is the mode of his self-offering.

But we can go deeper. Eucharistic gratitude is the Christological content of the mystery of God, because it reveals to us the depths of his inner-Trinitarian life. Eternally begotten by the Father, the Son lives out his perfect gift of self in return to the Father, in a mode of reception and gratitude. In this way, we can state that the mode of his sonship is his Eucharistic self-surrender. The Eucharist is given to us in sacramental form in order to transform us into sons and daughters in the Son. We do this through conformity to the Son's grateful reception of the gift of the Father, whose eternal love generates and sustains all of creation. The more Eucharistic we become, the more we are located in the Son and, thereby, divinized. The mystery of creation is now fully revealed as the Eucharistic form of God. That is why he was there, a hidden mystery in the dark corner of the Amalfi Cathedral. *Deus absconditus haic.*

When I earlier described the hills of the Cataract Ridge as everlasting, I meant it: they seemed never to end. I could hear wailing and grinding of teeth in the group with each passing hill; and knew that my words ("just one more hill to climb, guys") were viewed as nefarious shams, with a peasant revolt likely to ensue. In the heat of the long afternoon, the Sulfites were, like the wife of Lot, now completely turned into pillars of salt (cf. Gen 19:26).

And then we saw it. The ridge came to an end, and we looked down upon a small lake and our highest camp at just above 12,200 feet. There in the grassy knoll sat a few bursts of color, tents set up in advance by my lieutenants. The

far end of the lake collapsed at a cliff's edge, as an infinity pool; and, just beyond it, was the sight of all sights—
the Trinity Peaks. We had now reached the inner *sanctum*
of the San Juan Mountains. I simply cannot describe what
they are, other than to say how perfectly they express their
creator, the Trinity. Here the heart is simply ravished
by mystery, laid bare to offer the one thing necessary—
Eucharistic gratitude.

27

FATHERHOOD AND FAILURE

The Mountain West was first discovered in its depths. When the Spanish Explorer Juan Maria Antonio Rivera first entered the labyrinthian region of southwest Colorado in 1765, he did so by river. By the time the Escalante-Dominguez expedition followed a decade later, the river had acquired a mysterious name—Río de las Ánimas Perdidas en el Purgatorio (the River of the Lost Souls of Purgatory). Now known simply as the Animas River, its wild and seemingly aimless nature probes the depths of the San Juans. The river impressed itself on those first Spaniards, who thought themselves in Purgatory.

Our task that day was to go from heights to depths and then unto heights again. Starting at our high camp situated among the Needle Mountains, we would descend thousands of vertical feet to the Animas River and then ascend back to the high point of Molas Pass. It was our final day with the Sulfites as well as the final resupply of our month on the trail.

As we departed camp, the trail split: to the west, the Colorado Trail would pass toward the town of Silverton and then make its way south to its final destination in Durango; to the east, the Continental Divide Trail (unbroken from Georgia Pass) headed south, making its way for the Mexican border. Holding to the Colorado Trail, we passed westward into the Weminuche Wilderness—an expanse of unchartered terrain, nearly the size of Rhode Island. The guardians of the Weminuche were known as the Grenadiers, massive peaks of hardened quartzite, situated among the Vestal, Arrow, and Trinity Peaks. Just as the depths of the Animas were the first to be explored, the heights of these peaks were the last to be climbed.

Of all the adventures a man can take, there is none greater than fatherhood. This runs radically contrary to the modern ethos of backcountry culture, which cannot help but see marriage and family life as a deterrent. But within the Christian worldview, outdoor adventure serves a greater call—the adventure of a totally relational life, surrendered entirely in sacrificial love. The author Charles Péguy put it eloquently:

> There is only one adventurer in the world, as can be seen very clearly in the modern world, the father of a family. Even the most desperate adventurers are nothing compared with him. Everything in the modern world, even and perhaps most of all contempt, is organized against that fool, that imprudent, daring fool ... against the unruly, audacious man who is daring enough to have a wife and family.[1]

The father of the family is the adventurer par excellence, for his fatherhood is both generative and educative. The priest is likewise a father, but only in the latter sense, as a spiritual father and educator. Both share the joys and sorrows of "suffering through others", as Péguy puts it.

[1] Charles Péguy, "Clio I", in *Temporal and Eternal*, trans. Alexander Dru (London: Harvill Press, 1932), 108.

This is a radical reevaluation of the notion of adventure: in place of the individual pursuit of greatness, the purpose of fatherhood is to introduce children into the fullness of life and the discovery of their personhood in God. Granted, physical adventure is one of the great schools by which fathers form this way of life in their children, but always ordered toward the great spiritual adventure to God.

I had once heard it said that "fatherhood is only real when it is scorned." Whether it be true or not, it speaks of a key aspect to the adventure of fatherhood—the experience of failure. Because the father is a totally relational man, his limitations and failures are all the more pronounced, felt, and experienced by others. This is the source of great pain and suffering, in both children and fathers alike; and priests most certainly experience it. Without the knowledge of God as the Father and source of all, we cannot counter the culture's attempts to eliminate fatherhood.

As we passed those first miles in the Weminuche Wilderness, a painful memory came to mind. It happened just west of where we were, on a fourteener known as Wilson Peak. The mountain was made famous for being the logo of Coors Beer and rivals the Maroon Bells as the most iconic of all of Colorado's high peaks. It is also one of the most dangerous, because, situated on the far western side of the Rockies, its weather patterns are highly unpredictable. For this reason, its original Ute name is *Shandoka*, or "storm-maker".

The story always starts the same: too large a group, starting too late, moving too slowly up a fourteener. By the time we reached the final pitch of class 3 scrambling, thunder began to boom like cannon fire. We were now in trouble, and we were a very large group. The strong and sane descended in full spring; but some were panic-stricken and incapable of moving quickly. Fortunately, *Shandoka* only threatened that day, and the storm never broke upon us. We all safely descended to treeline, where I was left alone with my questioning doubts. There were so many signs that morning that we needed to turn back, even people telling me to do so. But in my self-reliance and excess of confidence, I pushed us on into circumstances that could have been tragic. It was a failure of judgment, on my part alone, and there was no way of excusing it—I had failed them as a father.

But thanks to Jesus Christ, we are not the sum total of our failures, and our fatherhood can be restored. The great gift of being a Christian is that all things are reconciled in God, so long as we surrender ourselves. Nothing is separated from the communion established by the Father in the atoning forgiveness of the Son. For in a stroke of utter paradox, God made the failure of the Cross the victory of the Resurrection. As Ratzinger explains:

> Did Jesus fail? Well, he certainly was not successful in the same sense as Caesar or Alexander the Great. From the worldly point of view, he did fail in the first instance: he died almost abandoned; he was condemned on account of his preaching. The response to his message was not the great Yes of his people, but the Cross. From such an end as that, we should conclude that Success is definitely not one of the names of God and that it is not Christian to have an eye to outward success or numbers. God's paths are other than that: his success comes about through the Cross and is always found under that sign ... it is not the Church of the successful people we find impressive ... what strengthens our faith, what remains constant, what gives us hope, is the Church of the suffering.[2]

[2]J. Ratzinger, *Collected Works*, vol. 11: *Theology of the Liturgy: The Sacramental Foundation of Christian Existence*, trans. John Saward, Kenneth Baker, Henry Taylor, et al. (San Francisco: Ignatius Press, 2014), 259–60.

The "failure" of the Cross reveals the interior depths and inner logic of the Christian life. As von Balthasar once said, it is "a marriage in poverty, and the cross is the marriage bed."[3] The mystery of the Cross is the mystery of divine love made poor, to the point of utter failure and total defeat in the eyes of the world. Success is not one of the names of God, and to attempt a "successful Christianity" is to eliminate the centrality of the Cross. Precisely in failure is love most evident, because being made poor for others is the basic truth of love. And from this the adventure of fatherhood begins.

Saint Ignatius of Loyola once described the Standard of Christ (the image of a military flag) under which his disciples are known: poverty, humiliation, and humility. By these three, he writes, we will be led to all other virtues. The inversion of this is the Standard of Satan, which is designated by the opposites: riches, honors, and pride. Upon these two standards is the battleground of the human heart, the arena upon which the drama of life unfolds.

The backcountry is a place of poverty, and for that reason we secretly pursue it. Cities give us a sense of comfort, security, and control, a place where it is easy never to feel failure. The modern world is built upon this false sense of safety, but one that does not satisfy the human heart. That's why fathers take the risk of sharing life with their children in the outdoors, in places of potential danger and powerlessness. We are drawn to lost rivers and forbidden peaks because deep down, we desire to be poor as God was made poor. "For you know the grace of our Lord Jesus Christ, that though he was rich, yet for your sake he became poor, so that by his poverty you might become rich" (2 Cor 8:9).

---

[3] H. U. von Balthasar, *You Crown the Year with Your Goodness: Radio Sermons*, trans. Graham Harrison (San Francisco: Ignatius Press, 1989), 39–40.

Following Christ, we must allow the experience of poverty to translate into humiliation and even contempt. We are now delving deeper into the mystery of love; for as von Balthasar writes, "love is only possible between humiliated human beings."[4] Only through the passageway of humiliation can we arrive at our final existential destination of humility. It is this virtue alone that befits the creature, and our entire relationship with God hinges on our ability to interiorize our creatureliness. But far from being deprecating or demeaning, humility is the freedom to live in the truth of reality. Only the soul steeped in humility has dismantled the illusions of one's achievements and power, "dispossessed of any self-constructed pattern of life".[5] Only then do we have the freedom to renounce the desire to control the course and trajectory of our lives. Humility is thereby a hallmark of an authentically human life and, thanks to the revelation of Christ, a distinctively Christian virtue. It alone makes possible true greatness, which is why Saint Thomas Aquinas pairs it with its complementary virtue—*magnanimitas*, or greatness of soul.

"Today only what is poor, interiorized, hidden—what is simple and true—can beneficially influence Christianity."[6] These words of von Balthasar harken to Christians in a secular age to embrace more profoundly the Standard of Christ. They call upon us to choose poverty so as to build our lives upon the riches of Christ; to embrace humiliation so as to enter the pathway of true love; and to rejoice in humility, which opens our life anew to the reality of God and, thereby, the fulfillment of all our desires. This

[4] H. U. von Balthasar, *Science, Religion and Christianity*, trans. Hilda Graef (London: Burns and Oates, 1958), 151.

[5] *Hans Urs von Balthasar on the Spiritual Exercises*, trans. Thomas Jacobi and Jonas Wernet (San Francisco: Ignatius Press, 2019), 60.

[6] H. U. von Balthasar, "One Spirituality of the Church", in *Theology Digest* 10 (1962): 194.

is the adventure of fatherhood—so long as we embrace our failures.

By the time we reached the Animas River, the Sulfites had nearly dissolved. One guy, known as "peg leg", had such severe knee pain that his every step looked as if his leg were disconnecting from his hip. We had a foreboding encounter with search-and-rescue, in pursuit of a climber missing for several days. The rope that bonded our group was clearly fraying, and we were nowhere near finished. During Mass by the river, a narrow-gauge train passed by, and I saw a few of them contemplating a jump aboard for a risky but free lift to town.

As with every group before, I wondered if we had pushed them too far. Then the rains came, suddenly and with great intensity. With 4.7 miles and 2,600 feet to climb out of the Animas basin and up to Molas Pass, I thought this would be the death blow to the Sulfites. But they rallied and charged the cliff walls with the war cries of madmen. But they were far from mad—they were now poor. And through their failures they had persevered and were now to celebrate the completed segment of the trail in the renewed bond of brotherhood. The adventure of these days together had made them glorious failures like their Master: poor, despised, and rejected. But they were raised in glory like the Son—and someday, they, too, would become fathers.

28

A LIFE IS A FORM

To walk the dusty streets of Silverton, Colorado, is to step back in time. A once bustling and vibrant mining town, it is now a booming metropolis of 662 people. But nestled in a picturesque valley just below 9,400 feet, the town comes back to life every summer, being, as it is, the heart of the San Juans. Each day a steam locomotive from the 1920s pulls into town from the Durango-Silverton Narrow-Gauge Railroad (the same the Sulfites almost jumped on yesterday). Tourists pour out of railcars and into shops, while mountain enthusiasts hang around in their vagabond manner. All feel the draw of this hidden and bygone mountain locale. But for the southbound Colorado Trail thru-hiker, Silverton signals something else—it is civilization's last outpost. With only seventy-five of the 486-mile trail remaining, this place gives one the first real sense that the end of the trail is near.

For the thru-hikers, this called for a preemptive celebration. We swaggered into the Handlebar Saloon to meet our last group, known as "the Boys". This group was a collection of our closest friends, for whom we reserved the final stretch of the trail. We thought they would be happy to see us. But on their faces, we only saw shock.

After twenty-seven days in the backcountry, tattered clothing and sunburnt faces were matched by a basic inability to adhere to social norms. Food and drink were not consumed—they were assaulted. But the reason for this savage comportment was not (solely) a lack of virtue; it was due to a backpacking phenomenon known as "hiker hunger".

Thru-hiking is a steady exercise at an aerobic intensity. But when it is compounded over weeks, the caloric depletion and maximal strain on the body produce a remarkable physiological change. This is accompanied by a psychological response that basically puts you in survival mode. In short, after several weeks of a thru-hike, one goes into "hiker hunger", where no matter how much you eat, you cannot stop being hungry. By this point, the body is convinced you are trying to kill it—so its every calorie must be stored away as a tactic of self-preservation.

Given our overindulgence that night, there was little enthusiasm for the trail the next morning. Molas Pass was rainy and cold, and we were now heading into another four days of remote backcountry. To the west and south of Silverton one finds expansive mountain basins linked by unnamed passes. We were traversing a unique geological formation, known as Hermosa, which 300 million years ago came to be as part of the Ancestral Rockies. As the clouds passed, the primordial beauty of our surroundings lifted our spirits and carried our tired bodies, providing a welcomed distraction from our hunger.

As the body adapts to the trail, so too does the soul begin to clarify. It could be described as "spiritual hiker hunger", which feeds, not on calories, but on meaning. On the trail, I become acutely aware of how I see things, of what is going on inside of me. I'm not busy or distracted—only present to that which is before me. From here comes a deeper contemplation of the "why" questions in life and, through them, a new consciousness at the level of world-view. Instead of just living, I now consider the very experience of life.

For the Christian, clarity of soul on the trail translates as follows: allowing my human experiences in creation to be inserted more deeply into the mystery of God. As we have seen throughout, these three themes—humanity, creation, and God—are drawn together in the singular mystery of the Incarnation. It alone is the center upon which the Christian worldview orbits, the interpretive key to our total vision of the real. But it can be considered a different way, namely, as a *form of life*.

Before delving into the idea that "life is a form", we need to make two preliminary remarks. First, living in a secular postmodern world, the Church can no longer afford to present the Christian faith as an aggregate of moral and doctrinal regulations. For so many young people, Christianity is simply a "bunch of rules and ideas" having no bearing on life whatsoever. Christianity must be "given back its strength in *us*", as De Lubac says, which means first and foremost that we discover its pure and authentic form.[1] Only through this can it again resonate in the things of life. Then, faith is no longer a private and compartmentalized aspect of my life; it becomes the totalizing form of everything. And this is the utmost human experience, as Ratzinger aptly describes: "Because being a Christian does not mean some special skill alongside other skills but simply the correct living out of being human, we could also say that we want to practice the skill of living correctly: we want to learn better the skill of skills, the art of being human."[2]

---

[1] H. de Lubac, *The Drama of Atheist Humanism*, trans. Edith M. Riley, Anne Englund Nash, and Mark Sebanc (San Francisco: Ignatius Press, 1995), 127.

[2] J. Ratzinger, *The Yes of Jesus Christ: Exercises in Faith, Hope, and Love*, trans. Robert Nowell (New York: Crossroad, 2016), 3.

If I were to summarize everything we were attempting on the Colorado Trail, it would be with these words from Joseph Ratzinger—to learn anew the art of being human. But the art form comes from the artisan himself, the God-Man, Jesus Christ. In becoming man in the Incarnation, he teaches us what it means to be human. In him alone do we find the lost art of being able to live. Or in the words of Blessed Pier Giorgio Frassati, "only faith gives us the possibility of living."[3]

Additionally, modern man must fight against the fragmentation of human life. His primary work of art is rediscovering the whole in the fragments, and the fragments in the whole. A secular worldview that nullifies God and eclipses the spiritual can never recover the whole; it leaves us only with fragments. The Christian of the post-Christian age can then offer the most astonishing of gifts: the real possibility of fragmented meaning in the meaning of the whole. We must first see the Christian faith as an original whole before applying it to our life. In the humanity of Christ, God gives us "the way" (Jn 14:6). Upon this path we tread, finding ourselves through the art of being human.

It is difficult to think of life as a form. But imagine for a moment that you are looking at an aspen tree in fall color. Illuminated by an autumnal light and trembling in soft wind, it radiates a kind of beauty and utter uniqueness that catches you off guard, that enraptures you. What you are experiencing is not a conglomerate of deciduous tree parts—you are seeing a *form*. As we discussed earlier, what you behold is a form, or *Gestalt*, as von Balthasar calls it. You are perceiving a hidden interior form within the being in front of you. As von Balthasar explains, "form is

[3] P. G. Frassati, *Letters to His Friends and Family*, trans. Timothy E. Deeter (Ann Arbor: Alba House, 2009), 155.

by definition the expression of the interior", an inner reality that is communicating itself through its exterior presence.[4] When we experience any *Gestalt*, we first perceive
it and, then, are enraptured. This is how beauty trans-
ports us—even wounds us—in ways we don't understand.
The heart awakens through the perception of form and is
utterly enraptured by it. It is the story of every romance
and any great human life. Beauty is not in the eye of the
beholder; the beholder is taken captive by the loving presence of the beautiful.

But to understand the true *Gestalt* of created things, we
must first interpret it according to its source. Creation is
not a whole; it is fragmented. God alone is the true whole,
the fullness from which everything lives. But God is not
known apart from Jesus Christ, who enters the world as a
concrete man in a historical time. For von Balthasar, this is
the point of departure, perhaps his principal contribution:
that "Jesus Christ is clearly a form" and that he "enters the
stage of history *in a form*".[5] Unless we view all of God's
self-disclosure in revelation under the total vision of its
Christological form, we simply cannot understand who
God is. The loss of this in the modern world is why we
think of Christianity as a content of ideas and rules, not the
radiant and enrapturing form of divine love.

Von Balthasar can now turn to us and pose the question:
"What is a person without a life-form, that is to say, without
a form which he has chosen for his life, a form into which
and through which to pour out his life?"[6] Man is unique
in creation, because unlike the aspen tree, which possesses

---

[4] H.U. von Balthasar, *Explorations in Theology*, vol. 4: *Spirit and Institution*,
trans. Edward T. Oakes, S.J. (San Francisco: Ignatius Press, 1995), 49.

[5] Ibid., 53 and 58.

[6] H.U. von Balthasar, *The Glory of the Lord: A Theological Aesthetics*, vol. 1,
Seeing the Form, 2nd ed., trans. Erasmo Leiva-Merikakis (San Francisco: Ignatius
Press, 2009), 23–24.

a form, man has the capacity of self-determination. But he only finds himself by embracing a form of life; his decisional moment, his sole defense against disintegration. This is why we stepped onto the Colorado Trail—to recover our form of life, that indissoluble interiority that makes my presence in the world truly unrepeatable.

But this all hinges on a final step—the Yes and No to Jesus Christ. There is no neutrality to the God question; not to answer is to have answered. The Gospel mandate is simple yet formidable: I either attempt to self-construct my own form from the fragments of my life, or I renounce my life and take on the form of Christ. Only the latter is a real form, because it alone possesses the whole. In this way, we can say with von Balthasar, "to be a Christian is precisely a form ... the most beautiful thing that may be found in the human realm."[7] Learning to see the Christian life as a form is only the beginning; now we commence the true project in every life—the art of being human.

After twenty miles and 4,000 feet of elevation gain, we at last ascended Bolas Pass and, from there, saw a truly incredible sight. To the west was the Wilson group of fourteeners, centered upon a towering spire known as Lizard Head. But beyond these final solitary peaks, we viewed for the first time the world beyond the Rockies. We had passed through the mountains and now beheld the high desert expanse of Utah. We were now turning south—fully south—into our last stretch of the trail and final destination in Durango.

As my eyes moved from the horizon to my more immediate surroundings, I realized that we had spent the entire day passing through wildflowers. But these were no

[7] Ibid., 27–28.

ordinary groves; they were massive, waist deep, spread to infinity all around us. Each flower had its own form, its particular *Gestalt*. Each communicated something of its life, speaking to us with interior radiance, saying, "I am totally unique in the universe."

That evening in the alpine garden, I gazed westward to the world beyond the mountains. All illusions passed away, and I was left alone with the real. I recalled the words of von Balthasar: "I find myself within the realm of a world and in the boundless community of other existent beings [that] is astonishing beyond measure and cannot be exhaustively explained by any cause which derives from within the world."[8] I knew in that moment that the sole purpose of my life was to discover the source of such infinite meaning—and that I could only find that in the form of God. And I no longer felt hungry.

---

[8] As quoted in *Hans Urs von Balthasar on the Spiritual Exercises*, ed. Jacques Servais, trans. Thomas Jacobi and Jonas Wernet (San Francisco: Ignatius Press, 2019), 15.

29

FIAT

Today was the last barnburner. At twenty-three miles and 4,000 feet of elevation, it was to be not just our last long day—it was our longest day on the trail. We set out from Bolas Lake and continued our southbound journey, mostly holding to the ridgeline of the South Hermosa Mountains. To the east was the resort of Purgatory; to the west, the old mining town of Rico. But these were not to be our destination, only two pillars through which we would pass.

After seventeen miles, we were assaulted by the worst storm we had seen on the trail. It was nothing short of an absolute and torrential downpour, the kind proper to the San Juan Mountains. Already drenched by the first round and seeing that the storm was settling in for the day, we stumbled our way into the forest of Orphan Butte. Indeed, we had become "orphans of the storm", to quote the novelist Evelyn Waugh.[1] We tucked under a huge piñon pine that looked like it had been transplanted from Middle Earth; beneath its extensive branches, we found a dry vestibule for shelter. Here we pitched our rain fly, and the seven of us settled in as evening drew near.

Defeated by the storm and soaked to the core, we contemplated whether it would be possible to finish the day.

---

[1] E. Waugh, *Brideshead Revisited* (Boston: Little, Brown and Company, 2012), 261.

But there was a problem—no water until Deer Creek, six miles ahead. We determined to stay in our tent, say Mass, and drink some hot chocolate. And then we would determine our fate.

After twenty-nine days on the Colorado Trail, I was starting to miss the feminine. It may sound strange coming from a priest, but every man, in every state in life, enjoys the companionship of women. Women bring to the world of man something extraordinarily unique, and life is not the same without them. Our decision to limit the Colorado Trail hike just to men was intentional, but certainly not the norm. For my twenty-year tenure in the backcountry had always been among adventurous women of faith, who participated in a decidedly feminine fashion. Too often in the mountains one meets women who are trying to be men; who in the attempt to prove something, end up losing themselves. Sadly, they have fallen victim to the "specifically masculine madness of our secularized age", as Gertrud von le Fort observed.[2] But not so the women we knew; they were brave, intrepid, and strong—but precisely *as* women. They were remarkable because they possessed the key; they knew and modeled their lives on Mary, the Mother of God.

For many, the Catholic emphasis on Mary seems to be in contradiction to the universal centrality of Jesus Christ. But this is not so: Jesus Christ is most certainly the center of history, undeniably the answer to every human question. He is a Divine Person, who entered creation by assuming a human nature. And the way that he did this is what draws unique attention to the person of Mary. Just as

---

[2] G. von le Fort, *The Eternal Woman: The Timeless Meaning of the Feminine,* trans. Marie Cecilia Buehrle (San Francisco: Ignatius Press, 2010), 18.

you cannot have God without Christ, you cannot understand Christ apart from his being "born of a woman" (Gal
4:4). A woman gave him his humanity, his very DNA.
She is then, not just a Christian example, but indispensable
and intrinsic to the very way in which God restored his
relationship to creation.

This is even more coherent when we view salvation
history as a whole. For the first chapter of Genesis to the
last in the book of Revelation is the story of *biblical woman.*
She takes different forms: first there is Eve, the primordial
woman; then the people of Israel, known as Daughter Zion.
After centuries of prefigurement, we at last arrive at the center of history and see Mary, the Mother of God. In her,
the Church is born, initiating the New Covenant that will
last for the rest of history. In the end times, biblical woman
takes apocalyptic form, where she flees into the wilderness
to a place God has prepared for her (cf. Rev 12:6).

Viewed from this vantage point of biblical woman, we
see what the Church Fathers discovered a century after
Christ: that just as Jesus is the new Adam (1 Cor 15:22),
so too is Mary the new Eve. She does not accomplish
the atoning redemption of man—that belongs to her Son
alone. But she participates in her uniquely feminine way
with her silent *yes* at the foot of the Cross. She is, then,
as Ratzinger describes, essential for our understanding of
biblical revelation and creation as a whole: "The figure
of the woman is indispensable for the structure of biblical
faith. She expresses the reality of creation as well as the
fruitfulness of grace.... To deny or reject the feminine
aspect of belief, or, more concretely, the Marian aspect,
leads finally to the negation of creation and the invalida-
tion of grace."[3]

---

[3] J. Ratzinger, *Daughter Zion: Meditations on the Church's Marian Belief,* trans.
John M. McDermott, S.J. (San Francisco: Ignatius Press, 1983), 27–28.

In our day, we have been told that Christianity is oppressively patriarchal because God is named father (and not mother). But divine paternity must be understood analogously, in a way that totally transcends our understanding of fatherhood. God's paternity belongs to the order of self-gift—he is father because he is the originating source of all reality. Furthermore, God assumes a male human nature in Jesus Christ, a decided fact of his self-disclosure. Does this then malign and diminish woman? Anyone who knows the content of Christian faith understands that it is precisely the opposite: Woman is ennobled in Christ and revealed in her fullness.

Woman's genius lies, not in her initiating self-gift, but in her receptive self-giving. She is, in the words of the author Berdyaev, "the answering love of man to the infinite divine love".[4] She is not merely equal in dignity to man, but complementary in the order of self-gift. But she is more: precisely as feminine, she expresses the reality of creation. But how so? Here we return to our earlier metaphysical survey. What defines creation is that it is not from itself, but from God. It thereby stands in a relational and receptive mode. Woman has always been called the crown jewel of creation because, being receptive in body and surrendered in soul, she is the key to understanding creation.

Perhaps the pagans were onto something when they spoke of "mother earth". For truly, the motif of woman echoes throughout all of creation. We cannot understand what creation is, or how we ourselves are creaturely, apart from the mystery of woman. And if we cannot know God apart from creation, then we can conclude with Louis Bouyer: "Man needs woman in order to encounter God."[5]

---

[4] N. Berdyaev quoted in von le Fort, *Eternal Woman*, xvii.

[5] L. Bouyer, *Woman in the Church*, trans. Marilyn Teichert (San Francisco: Ignatius Press, 1984), 58.

Two thousand years ago, a young virgin in the town of Nazareth received a singular grace: she was to be the Mother of God and the concrete personalization of biblical woman. The etymological roots of her name "Mary" come from *myrm*, meaning "height" or "summit" in the ancient language of Ugaritic.[6] In her we glimpse the heights of creation and the summit of humanity. But this exalted place was a grace, the gift of God given for the mission of being his mother. Her singular grace, an objective gift that enveloped her whole life from the moment of her conception, permitted her to offer a subjective response, a total Yes of receptive and surrendering assent. We see this manifested when the Angel announces the call to bear the God-man. Her response? "Behold, I am the handmaid of the Lord; let it be to me according to your word" (Lk 1:38). It is within this "let it be" (*fiat* in Latin) that we glimpse the truth of creation and the essence of what it means to be in relation with God.

Because Mary's life is a perfect unity of objective grace and subjective assent, she becomes the archetypal disciple of Christ. She is not called to be an apostle or to represent Christ in hierarchical office. For she is greater: Mary does not represent the Church, she *is* the Church. She is, as Augustine says, *mundus reconciliatus Ecclesia* (the Church: the world reconciled to God).[7] Mary then stands at the heart of the Church, as the Church, offering her perfect *fiat* of loving surrender to the Father. Every Christian is then Marian; or, more precisely, to be Christ in created form is to be Mary. In this way she does not conflict with

[6] E. Sri, *Rethinking Mary in the New Testament* (Augustine Institute—San Francisco: Ignatius Press, 2018), 5.

[7] Augustine, as cited in H. de Lubac, *Splendor of the Church*, trans. Michael Mason (San Francisco: Ignatius Press, 1986), 184.

the mission of Jesus, but mirrors his perfect, eternal reception of the Father's love in created form.

At one point on the Colorado Trail, we celebrated the feast of Our Lady of Mount Carmel. During the opening prayer of the Mass, I prayed these words: "Father, may the prayers of the Blessed Virgin Mary, Mother and Queen of Carmel, protect us and bring us to your holy Mountain, Christ our Lord, who lives and reigns with you and the Holy Spirit, God, for ever and ever. Amen."

Christ is the mountain, and Mary is the guide. Her *fiat* was given, not just for her, but on behalf of all creation. In her we see that the fullness of woman reveals the perfection of creation. Every Christian is called to offer his own *fiat* of "letting things be" within this perfect Marian *fiat* that brought God into the world. And women, precisely as women, embody and ennoble this in their totally unique and beautifully feminine way. This, Charles Péguy calls the "Marian measure".[8] And it is the only way to understand the truth of creation and the reality of the Church.

We need women to be women, and we need them to be holy like Mary. As Léon Bloy once wrote, *plus une femme est saint, plus elle est femme* (the more a woman is a saint, the more she is a woman).[9] Without their presence, we would never be able to glimpse the Church as she truly is. Far from being an antiquated institution run exclusively by men, the Church *is* Mary and Mary *is* the Church. For her own part, woman will never come to know the truth of her beauty unless she participates in the maternal mission of Mary. As Louis Bouyer writes: "The mystery of woman, precisely because it is the mystery of creation

[8] C. Péguy quoted in H. U. von Balthasar, *The Glory of the Lord: A Theological Aesthetics*, vol. 1, *Seeing the Form*, 2nd ed., trans. Erasmo Leiva-Merikakis (San Francisco: Ignatius Press, 2009), 354.

[9] L. Bloy quoted in von le Fort, *Eternal Woman*, 51.

redeemed, completed and espoused by God himself, presupposes the mystery of God and cannot be understood without reference to him."[10]

The mystery of woman stands or falls with the mystery of God. So, too, with the mystery of creation, which hinges on woman's living out her femininity in Marian fullness. In Mary, creation reaches its absolute height—it is, as Gertrud von le Fort says, "the solitary flower of the mountains, far up at the fringe of eternal snows".[11] Only from this vista can we understand the meaning of creation in God, and only women can show us the way.

After several hours under the tent, with the storm unrelenting, we finally embraced our fate and decided to finish the day. For six of the longest miles of the Colorado Trail we were hammered by rain, chastened by lightning, and, all and all, embittered by the trail.

But at last we made it to Deer Creek, pitched wet tents, and climbed into warm sleeping bags. We did so in haste, which evidently caused a disturbance. For the first time in a month, we had arrived in the dark at a site that was almost entirely occupied by other groups. Apparently, we were an imposition, laughing loudly over a cribbage game late in the evening. An altercation followed, where members of another group came to tell us off. But one look at Casey's biceps, and they quietly returned to their tents.

This day would not be counted as our favorite, though it was indeed memorable. And now approaching the penultimate day of the trail, anticipation began to build. The last barnburner was complete, and now only two easy days

[10] Bouyer, *Woman in the Church*, 29.

[11] Von le Fort, *Eternal Woman*, 26. The quote, specifically about consecrated virgins, applies generally to the Marian Church.

kept us from the finish. Deer Creek to Junction Creek tomorrow, then the Kennebec Trailhead of Durango— and the end.

We had spent a month in a school of receptivity, taking each day as it came—weather, conditions, exposure, and the like. Perhaps this day was our deepest act of self-surrender, or then again, maybe it was another. Regardless, harsh weather in the backcountry has a way of making a *fiat* out of even the hardest of men. For if the trail teaches one thing, it is the Marian posture of trustful surrender.

30

LOVE—A WILDERNESS

Though the storms continued through the night, the morning dawn awoke with warm freshness and dry vigor. Clouds held to the valleys below, gesturing rapidly upon the high peaks, veiling and unveiling the mysterious scenery before us. Only sixteen miles and 2,600 feet of elevation stood between us and our final campground at Junction Creek. But work remained. Once gaining the Indian Trail Ridgeline, we would hold to this spin-like passage and continue on its very long traverse.

As we ascended Blackhawk Pass, I saw the La Plata Mountains. This small subrange of the San Juans, a final collection of high peaks in the state, was the last through which we would pass. The peaks were nothing short of stunning: Snowstorm, a rounded cirque of intense magnitude; Sharkstooth, as its name suggests, a razor-sharp geological feature. But the most beautiful was Hesperus, called by the Navajo *Dibé Ntsaa*—the Sacred Mountain of the North. Its alternating stripes of black and white granite could well have been the prototype of Italian Romanesque-Gothic architecture, as one sees most strikingly in Siena.

We at last descended the long ridge of Indian Trail, arriving at the pristine tranquility of Taylor Lake. From here, we saw our last pass, the final ascent of our nearly 500-mile journey. But it was then that the thunderstorms returned.

On a rock by the side of Lake Lucerne in the summer of 1943, Hans Urs von Balthasar composed a masterpiece entitled *Heart of the World*. Described by many as "the most cultivated of his time", he wrote more books than some people read in their lifetime.[1] But at the heart of his mountainous corpus is a poetic gem, a meditation on the heart of Jesus as it continues to pulse throughout creation. It is the most beautiful book I have ever read, and its last chapter, "Love—A Wilderness", is the central lens by which I have studied God in the backcountry. "O the blessed wilderness that is your love!" he begins, "no one will ever be able to subdue you, no one explore you."[2] To encounter the love of God is to step into a wilderness, a wild place that we cannot control and cannot tame. For though God has revealed his inner depths in Christ, knowledge of him remains all the more unknowable, a fiercely wild frontier of unfathomable beauty.

When we first discover the living God, we naturally seek the safe assurance of a path, the reliability of a trail. But as the years pass, we come to see that we are being led deeper into the wild. As von Balthasar describes:

> When I was still young I thought one could come into the clear with you. I saw a steep road ahead of me and I felt my courage swell. So I fastened my knapsack and began to climb.... But today, after all these years, when I lift up

[1] Cf. H. de Lubac, *The Church: Paradox and Mystery*, trans. James R. Dunne and Anne Englund Nash (San Francisco: Ignatius Press, 2021), 148.

[2] H. U. von Balthasar, *Heart of the World*, trans. Erasmo S. Leiva (San Francisco: Ignatius Press, 1979), 204.

my eyes, I see your dazzling pinnacles towering over me higher and more unreachable than ever. And I have long since stopped talking about a road.[3]

In our early years with God, we desire to make him known. We equip ourselves with the regional maps of the spiritual life and all the gear afforded by the tradition. We look to measure success according to the cairns of moral conversion, to confirm our location in dogmatic designations. But as we climb, divine love becomes only more incomprehensible. We feel the vertiginous loss of our frail human knowledge and are confronted with the challenge of a new surrender: "One day I threw everything in the bushes—knapsack, provisions and map—and I consecrated myself to you alone, O virginal landscape, and I became free for you."[4]

The Catholic tradition has always held a balance between what is called the *via positiva* and the *via negativa*. The former refers to the fact we can say things positively about God—He is good, He is love, etc. In Jesus Christ, God has been truly revealed, which means that dogmatic truths affirmed by the Church are timeless and real. But the latter, one that we often miss, is the deeper and more powerful dimension of Christian faith, the "negative". Because God infinitely transcends human words, they never capture him. For this reason, we must deny anytime we assert. When I say "God is good" or "God is love", I must say he is "not good" and "not love", because he radically defies my comprehension of these concepts. These "negative" statements about God are not denials or contradictions; they are simply the logic of analogy, an admission of creaturely limitation.

[3] Ibid.
[4] Ibid., 205.

The Church clarified this theological balance in the thirteenth century: "For between creator and creature there can be noted no similarity so great that a greater dissimilarity cannot be seen between them."[5] This "greater dissimilarity" is the *via negativa*, also known as the apophatic. Words truly express the nature of God; but they never fully capture the reality. Every word we utter about God is a garden—cultivated, ordered, pristine. But the reality beyond that word is a wilderness—untamed, ungraspable, and truly wild.

We never move beyond the positive, beyond the dogma and praxis of the Church. The Church is a fact, a historical reality founded by Jesus Christ to extend his life to every time and every place. Her one task is the faithful transmission of his truth and life, and she fulfills this role by the supernatural presence of the Holy Spirit. But as his bride and our mother, the Church always invites us to the divine wilderness beyond, to the endless vistas each dogmatic vantage point provides. She is bound by the total mystery of God, who, though revealing himself, remains always a mystery. In the words of Saint Augustine: *Sic comprehendis, non est Deus* (If you understand it, it is not God).[6]

Now affirming the incomprehensibility of God within our true knowledge of him does not lead to a kind of buddhistic *nada*, but it does refashion the way we approach him. It fosters a kind of transcendental reverence, one that is needed more than ever in our techno-scientific world. The path to God passes by way of the cross, the culminating moment of powerlessness and non-comprehension. Allowing the cruciform nature of God's self-disclosure to impress

[5] Fourth Lateran Council, Constitution, no. 2.
[6] Augustine, *Sermon 117*.

itself upon us means renouncing our attempts to control him and reduce him to an object. Many people speak of God like they speak of anything else—he is a good thing in my life, like my best friend or favorite kind of pizza. Certainly, they mean more than this, but without this deeper acceptance of the total "unknowability" of God, we reduce Christ to a caricature and God to an idea.

To experience the love of God as a wilderness is the only pathway to true knowledge of him. And much of this comes through suffering. It is in the moments when our life is shipwrecked on the cliff shores of reality that our hearts must expand to a place of uncomprehending trust. Von Balthasar affirms this path: "Only through the experience of suffering does man acquire true knowledge of God and of himself."[7] But this is too hard for us to hear, too much to bear (cf. Jn 6:60). Only with the grace of God can we surrender the titanic struggle to "overcome" and sublimate our suffering. To walk the path of powerless love is truly to become a disciple of our crucified Lord.

Through the dark night of the cross we come to the dawn of the resurrection. The wilderness "beyond" is not empty and perilous—it is a world transfigured by the Resurrected Christ. Within this event, our vision of reality is completely transformed. Everything is now an event in the sphere of love. Or, as von Balthasar describes: "The reality of creation as a whole has become a monstrance of God's real presence."[8] It is in this moment that life has been transfigured and the world in which I live

---

[7] H. U. von Balthasar *The Glory of the Lord: A Theological Aesthetics*, vol. 1, *Seeing the Form*, 2nd ed., trans. Erasmo Leiva-Merikakis (San Francisco: Ignatius Press, 2009), 256.

[8] H. U. von Balthasar, *The Glory of the Lord: A Theological Aesthetics*, vol. 2: *Studies in Theological Style: Clerical Styles*, trans. Andrew Louth, Francis McDonagh, and Brian McNeil, C.R.V. (San Francisco: Ignatius Press, 1984), 420.

truly re-created. It was this that Dostoevsky described the night that Alyosha saw creation as the wilderness of divine love:

> The vault of heaven, full of soft, shining stars, stretched vast and fathomless above him. The Milky Way ran in two vast streams from the zenith to the horizon. The fresh, motionless, still night enfolded the earth. The white towers and golden domes of the cathedral gleamed out against the sapphire sky. The gorgeous autumn flowers, in the beds round the house, were slumbering till morning. The silence of earth seemed to melt into the silence of the heavens. The mystery of earth was one with the mystery of the stars ... Alyosha stood, gazed, and suddenly threw himself down on the earth.[9]

We have come now to the essence of sanctity. The saint is not a rectified moralist who never makes mistakes; he is a person consummated in divine love. Like Alyosha, he sees creation as the ultimate monstrance of the unknowable God. He has trodden the ever-fading path that leads to the heart of God. He has been made poor in love, because he has tasted something beyond this world. Thus the saint alone is the true "spokesman of creation".[10]

The wild nature of saintly love seems impossible to us. So, too, does the wilderness of divine love seem too intimidating, too impossible. The world seems to have lost so much, and hope seems to be fleeting as with the setting sun. But as von Balthasar reminds us: "The true peaks rise as the distance grows; we must take care not to consider

---

[9] F. Dostoevsky quoted in W. Lynch, *Christ and Apollo: The Dimensions of the Literary Imagination* (Wilmington: ISI Books, 2004), 32–33.

[10] R. Guardini, *The Art of Praying: The Principles and Methods of Christian Prayer*, trans. Prince Leopold of Loewenstein-Wertheim (Manchester, NH: Sophia Institute Press, 1995), 58.

our own age as an age without salvation or saints."[11] Let us join their ranks, stepping out into the incomprehensible wilderness of divine love.

The beauty of the moment offered asylum from the coming storm. There we stood, at the top of Kennebec Pass—the ultimate climb of the Colorado Trail—gazing upon the last vista and our final frontier. For 7,000 feet below us, we saw the town of Durango, illuminated in glory as if in a dream.

Durango, Colorado, is the third installment of its namesake. Founded in 1880 by railroad entrepreneurs headed for Silverton, it was designated by Governor Alexander Hunt after his visit to Durango, Mexico. This Mexican Durango, dating back to 1563, received its name from the town of northern Spain, which we can trace back to at least the eleventh century. In its most ancient form, the word "Durango" comes from the Basque *Urango*, or "place of water". The Durango we saw from the heights of Kennebec was not simply the water town of the Animas River—it was a glimpse of the heavenly Jerusalem, with "the river of the water of life" (Rev 22:1).

That long descent, matched by the pounding of continual rain, was the final blow we would take in our month-long bout with the Colorado Trail. But as we arrived at our final camp near Junction Creek, the storm subsided and the evening spirits lifted. It was then that something strange happened—we started to feel sentimental. Beneath the enthusiasm of tomorrow's finish, there was the ache that we were leaving the trail. Our journey was ending,

---

[11] H. U. von Balthasar, *Razing the Bastions: On the Church in This Age*, trans. Brian McNeil, C.R.V. (San Francisco: Ignatius Press, 1993), 32.

our fellowship disbanding. Never again would the four of us experience anything like this.

As men do when they feel sentimental, we went fishing. That night, we caught Rio Grande cutthroat, the Colorado state fish and the most beautiful I have ever seen. In the company of "the Boys", banter assuaged our melancholy and laughter kept things light. We had spent a month in the backcountry on a trip we would never forget. Tomorrow we would step back into civilization and begin again an urban adventure in the wilderness of divine love.

31

UNTO DEPTHS

For the past thirty days we had traveled through eight mountain ranges, six national forests, and five major river systems, scaled 90,000 feet of elevation, and traversed 486 of the beautiful and rugged miles on the American continent. Now this chapter of life, our adventure on the Colorado Trail, was coming to a close. Waking late on that final morning, we drank coffee with the same solemnity as we had on our first day on the trail. All things come to an end, and just when we think we have grasped the present, it belongs to the past.

Recall the character we met on Sargents Mesa, whose tent nearly caught fire from the thunderstorm. We met him this morning at Junction Creek and heard his story. He, too, had been thru-hiking for the month, with no communication back home. When he arrived in Silverton several days ago, there was a letter waiting for him at the post office from his wife: a family member had died, and he had missed the funeral while on the trail. Being a faithful Catholic, he joined us for our final Mass, which I offered for his faithful departed. During the Eucharistic Prayer, I was reminded why we were out here: "That we might live no longer for ourselves, but for him who died and rose again for us." All things, even human life, must come to an end.

The purpose of the thru-hike was to teach us how truly to live—and that means death to self and life in Christ. By doing it, I can affirm the primacy of a love that transcends the world. This whole grand school of creation, the place where we had learned the art of being human, was nothing more than a deep immersion in this divine love. And that is what we felt as we prayed together for a fellow soul passing into eternity.

The trail's end was drawing near, and we felt resistant to it. I now understand why so many thru-hikers can never leave it. For many, it offers an escape from life, from the pains of relationships and wounds of civilization. We all feel the temptation to wander endlessly the expanse of the backcountry. Everything feels more real on the trail, life so simple and beautiful. Truly, a thru-hike is life *intensified*.

But the trail requires a translation, one that interprets the material into the spiritual. And for those of us attempting the lifetime project of being a Christian, we knew it was to be found in the Incarnation. Without God becoming man in Jesus Christ, there is no warrant to leave the trail, no call to return to ordinary life. Without an overarching worldview steeped in the love of God, we can use the trail for our own purposes, a way of buffering us from reality. But this never satisfies. Once we grasp at the trail, we no longer receive it as a gift. With this in mind, we prepared our hearts for the final miles, for that moment when we would have to step off.

◆ ◆ ◆

In the early 1980s, Pope John Paul II would escape the Vatican and make his way north to the Alps. Here he would spend time in secret, hiking in the summers and skiing in the winters. An Italian alpinist named Lino Zani described a conversation he had had with the pope, after one such day.

> "Lino, who or what drives you to get to the top of those mountains, why do you do it?" I answered him: "Because I like to understand and discover what is beyond, and when I arrive up there at the top, it seems to me that I can understand. I have a different perspective on things." He said, "It's the same for me. We're both looking for the same thing, that's why we understand each other." But then he added, and I will never forget it, "But remember that when you get to the top, you can only go down. Man can only go so high!"[1]

Like Zani, we set out on the Colorado Trail primarily to make for the heights. How could we forget that first glimpse of Georgia Pass, when at last we stood above the trees? And what compares to that midnight memory on the top of San Luis, where we tasted Heaven? But now as the trail descended to the town of Durango, we too were challenged by the pope's words: "Now you can only go down. Man can only go so high!"

We are made, not just for the heights, but also for the depths. If we reject the latter, we become like Nietzsche, who despised the depths in his worship of the heights. As his *übermensch* proclaims, in a moment of total self-creation: "All that is deep shall rise up to my heights."[2] Idolatry of the heights is promethean defiance, an attempt at self-deification. *My* heights, says Nietzsche—and this says it all.

This stands in fundamental contradiction with the God of Jesus Christ, he to whom alone the heights belong.

---

[1] L. Zani and M. Simoneschi, *The Secret Life of John Paul II*, trans. Matthew Sherry (Charlotte, N.C.: Saint Benedict Press, 2012), 82.

[2] F. Nietzsche, "Thus Spoke Zarathustra", in *The Portable Nietzsche*, trans. Walter Kaufmann (New York: Penguin Books, 1954), 236.

As von Balthasar writes of the Incarnation, perhaps with Nietzsche in mind:

> What comes from above has no need of heights. It needs the depths; it longs to experience the abyss. What comes from above is already pure and protected; it can reveal itself only by a descent. What comes from below naturally strives for the heights. Its impulse presses on to the light; its impetus a seeking of power. Every finite spirit wants to assert itself and luxuriantly unfurl its leafy crown in the sun of existence.... Man wants to soar up, but the Word wants to descend. Thus the two meet half-way, in the middle, in the place of the Mediator.[3]

God descends because he loves the depths. He does this first in creation, that primordial "book" that speaks of his love. He lavishly squanders truth, goodness, and beauty in an act of sheer gift, setting man as the crown of his creation. Then when we reject him, he descends in an even more profound way—by becoming man and entering history. And this culminates in the most definitive act in the drama of history: the Cross, death, and Resurrection of Christ. Within this he descends to the very depths of creation; to Hell and the rescue the souls, and only then in ascent to the heights of the Father. He knows all depths and draws them back to the heights. All that is left for us is, like Saint Catherine of Siena, to be astonished in love: "What an immeasurably profound love! Your Son went down from the heights of his divinity to the depths of our humanity. Can anyone's heart remain closed and hardened after this?"[4]

---

[3] H. U. von Balthasar, *Heart of the World*, trans. Erasmo S. Leiva (San Francisco: Ignatius Press, 1979), 38–39.

[4] Catherine of Siena, *Dialogues*, book 4, no. 13.

But the truest depths, those loved most intensely by God, are lost places in the human heart. As Léon Bloy writes, "Man has places in his heart which do not yet exist, and into them enters suffering, in order that they may have existence."[5] The cruciform love of Jesus, emptied in his descent, is the suffering that restores the human heart. All of our depths, even the darkest corners of our hearts, are laid bare to the God of the heights, in whose descent we see the final conquest of love.

The pattern of every Christian life is communion with God and a share in his mission. In the words of Saint Paul, it is simply a being "in Christ" (2 Cor 5:17). In him, we are called, not just to ascend to the heights of the Father, but to descend in him into the depths. In a way, the latter is the greater challenge: to become, like the Son, a man "who lives from the depths, and masters every moment from the depth."[6] Father Gawronski knew this and spoke it as a prophetic word during my first Mass homily:

> The fourteeners you have scaled are only the beginning, and they will have to disappear to reveal the true mountains to which they only point, the mountains of the soul.... Like John Paul, you will be able to get to the mountains for a long time to come, to refresh your soul—but your ministry, into the depths of human hearts, into the mystery of human relations, of that community which is the Body of Christ, will lead you far from the mountains, even as Jesus himself had to leave his beloved home country for the Holy City.... He will meet you, His disciple, at the true mountain.[7]

[5] L. Bloy quoted in G. Greene, *The End of the Affair* (London: Penguin Classics, 2004), title page.

[6] D. von Hildebrand, *The Art of Living* (Steubenville: Hildebrand Press, 2017), 14.

[7] R. Gawronski, *Islands of Humanity: The Writings of Father Raymond Gawronski, S.J. (1950–2016)*, vol. 2: *The First Mass Homilies* (self-published), 51.

For so many years of my life, I had been looking for God on mountain heights. Now as a priest, I knew that he had found me in the depths of my soul. And though I will spend the rest of my life in pursuit of the heights, I am no longer afraid of the depths—either of my heart or of those that I meet. For in Jesus Christ, the God-man, the heights and depths are one.

On a quiet afternoon of a forgotten day on the Colorado Trail, I sat by a creek reading T. S. Eliot with a fellow hiker. I knew then that the words I read that day would be my last—and with them, I concluded my final homily.

> We shall not cease from exploration
> And the end of all our exploring
> Will be to arrive where we started
> And know the place for the first time.
> Through the unknown, remembered gate
> When the last of earth left to discover
> Is that which was the beginning;
> At the source of the longest river
> The voice of the hidden waterfall
> And the children in the apple-tree
> Not known, because not looked for
> But heard, half-heard, in the stillness
> Between two waves of the sea.
> Quick now, here, now, always—
> A condition of complete simplicity
> (Costing not less than everything).[8]

In a few hours, we would "arrive where we started"—in the company of family and friends, in the civilized world of the twenty-first century. Adventures end, but exploration

[8] T. S. Eliot, *Four Quartets* (New York: HarperCollins, 1943), 59.

never dies. And now it was time to set out from our final camp and complete the trail.

I'm not sure who started it, but we began to run. It started as a slow jog and then became an all-out sprint. Thru-hikers at the front, the Boys behind, we ran the last five miles of the Colorado Trail as if they had been our first. All sadness had dissolved as the exhilaration of the finish drew near. Donning American flag shorts and wearing face paint, we ripped through those last miles without any thought of our heavy packs or even the slightest sense of our exhausted bodies. I heard screams—Casey and Cody had cut a switchback—and accidently ambushed a family as they reemerged from the woods. Excitement pitched, an anticipation on the verge of the unbearable. And then we saw the sign—the last mile.

We stopped. With every deep breath, we drew in the moment, knowing them to be our last. I looked at the men I was with, some of the greatest I will ever know. With Cody, Casey, and Luke, a month on the Colorado Trail was more friendship than some experience in a lifetime. But it was time to finish, and we were going to savor it. We walked that last mile slowly, with humility and confidence, embracing the last steps of the Colorado Trail. We had endured endless challenges, battled for the survival of so many groups, and now, it was time to rest.

When we turned the last corner, I saw my four nephews, standing in the midst of our families at the trail's end. In that moment, my adventure ended and theirs began. For the day would come when I would take them on the Colorado Trail. Then they, too, would discover their humanity in creation, and creation in God—leading them, in Jesus Christ, to heights and unto depths.

EPILOGUE

In 1923, Carl Blaurock and William Ervin completed the summits of Colorado's fourteeners. At the same time in the north of Italy, Romano Guardini published the first of his *Letters from Lake Como*, the principal inspiration of this book. Now 100 years later, just as I was completing this manuscript, I had one last Mass on a fourteener summit. But there was a problem—it was snowing.

It was only September 14th. But with an unusual Pacific hurricane sweeping inland, inauspicious weather conditions were assailing the Rockies. And they were wreaking havoc on my plan. For thirteen years, I had reascended the fourteeners, saying Mass on every summit. Years ago, my climbing partner Father Sean and I had determined we would finish with Mount of the Holy Cross on the feast of the Holy Cross—September 14th. But now stuck in a blizzard, it was simply not meant to be. In peace, we canceled the climb. There is always another day.

It has now been over a year since we stepped off the Colorado Trail. Luke and Cody had gone to seminary and, in a few years, would be priests. Casey, despite the vocational badgering of Cody, was set to marry "the white buffalo" the next fall. Occasionally we saw others from the trail—the Fellowship, Symposium, Kung Fu Pandas, Derping Corgis, Libertarians, Sulfites, and the Boys. They were always met with "the right hand of fellowship" (Gal 2:9), bonded forever as we were by the hardship of the trail. Seeing them reminds me of a poem by Tennyson:

Come, my friends,
'Tis not too late to seek a newer world ...
We are not now that strength which in old days
Moved earth and heaven, that which we are, we are;
One equal temper of heroic hearts,
Made weak by time and fate, but strong in will
To strive, to seek, to find, and not to yield.[1]

The Colorado Trail was not just an adventure; it was something forever woven into the fabric of our lives. As the years pass and our story finds its place in the halls of eternal memory, I become more aware of the great mystery we glimpsed in those heights and depths. But the story is far from over. As von Balthasar writes: "Perfection lies in fullness of journey. For this reason, never think you have arrived."[2]

Several months after the trail, I came across a line from G.K. Chesterton that seemed to summarize it all: "The soul of a landscape is a story and the soul of a story is a personality."[3] Creation is not made for itself; it is made for a story. And every story is about persons, about the human heart seeking meaning through the drama of life. But a Christian worldview interprets this more profoundly. As Ratzinger writes, "God created the world in order to enter into a history of love with mankind. In its very essence, his creative action is the action of history."[4]

[1] A.L. Tennyson, "Ulysses", in *The Works of Alfred Lord Tennyson* (New York: Grosset & Dunlap, 1892), 93–94.

[2] H.U. von Balthasar, *Heart of the World*, trans. Erasmo S. Leiva (San Francisco: Ignatius Press, 1979), 23.

[3] G.K. Chesterton, *The Everlasting Man* (San Francisco: Ignatius Press, 1993), 174.

[4] J. Ratzinger, *The Divine Project: Reflections on Creation and the Church*, trans. Chase Faucheux (San Francisco: Ignatius Press, 2023), 53.

Casey, Cody, Luke, and I were not the protagonists of the story of the Colorado Trail. The landscape of creation exists for the story of humanity, and the soul of that story is the personality of Jesus Christ. Our story of the trail, like every human story, is drawn into the metanarrative of all history. Von Balthasar calls this *Theo-Drama*: God the Father, the playwright and author of the story; the Holy Spirit, its director; and the Son, the central actor around which the drama unfolds. We Christians are invited onto the stage of Christ, to become his co-actors. Creation is the stage where the history of the *Theo-Drama* unfolds.

As moderns, it is difficult for us to see a unity to the creation of the world and the saving history of God. But the unity lies in the center, in the Incarnation: there we find the same *logos* of creation and redemption. God, who created the world in the Son, now re-creates it in him. The aspen trees and wildflowers will come and go with the passing of seasons; the mountains will endure the many centuries to come. But the short life of man is marked by a created capacity for God, one that makes him "like God" (cf. Gen 1:26). Amidst the baffling complexity of the created world, he is completely and utterly distinct. Man remains the only creature on earth that God willed for its own sake. In his body and soul, matter and spirit unite; in male and female form, God's self-giving love is imaged. A rational and free being, he alone contemplates and loves God in and through created things.

In light of this, let us briefly recall what we learned on the Colorado Trail.

1. Humanity longs to be immersed in creation. In it we discover the essence of our own being; that we are, in fact, created. Contrary to the illusory, techno-world of self-creation, we only find peace and rest for our souls by embracing our creatureliness. But this requires work: we must acknowledge limitations, embrace dependency, and

live in relationship to God. Only then is life lived in accordance with the logic of being. Guided by the Incarnate Lord, we set out to make authenticated humanity the hallmark of our Christian lives. Make man the way, and you shall arrive at God.

2. Creation, our metaphysical "native place", is not just our home—it is the place of the exploration of God. When we glimpse the *logos*, the meaningfulness of all creation, we discover it to be of inestimable richness. And what makes it all the more unbelievable is the recognition that *being* is in fact gift. In that sense, all is gift. A loving contemplation, steeped in Eucharistic gratitude, is the only fitting response and the source of enduring joy. In the words of von Balthasar: "Only the person who contemplates the beauty of nature in God and is accustomed to regard it as his voice, his sphere, the mirror of his countenance, can, even in his mature years, experience nature as naïvely and ecstatically as in his eighteenth year, without a drop of melancholy."[5]

3. God is made real again in the created humanity of Jesus. In the third chapter of Mark, our Lord establishes his method of discipleship by ascending the mountain: "Then he went up on to the mountainside, and called to him those whom it pleased ... to be his companions" (Mk 3:13, Knox Translation). Companionship with Christ is the way to union with God. We are to be his disciples, fed by the bread of his truth, and led ever more deeply into the mystery of the Father's love. For the heart and source of Jesus' life was a truth: *the will of the Father is the love of the Father.*[6] To be Christ's companions is to embrace this grounding reality; that only through obedience *in* the Son

---

[5] H. U. von Balthasar, *The Grain of Wheat: Aphorisms*, trans. Erasmo Leiva-Merikakis (San Francisco: Ignatius Press, 2011), 8.

[6] R. Guardini, *The Lord*, trans. Elinor Castendyk Briefs (Washington, D.C.: Regnery, 1954), 41.

do I come to a life lived in God. All else is shadows, the emptiness of passing things.

T.S. Eliot once wrote that "man cannot bear very much reality."[7] This may be so, but the contrary is true— man cannot bear *unreality*. The world in which we find ourselves is becoming increasingly unreal; relationships digitized by screens, nature manipulated into global corporatism, and truth reduced to the ideological functioning of the will to power. The Christian finds himself a stranger in a strange land, speaking a foreign language and despised as an alien. But steeped in the Incarnational worldview of Jesus Christ, he does not merely have something to say—he has everything to say. He alone knows the truth of humanity, immersed as it is in the reality of creation. To him alone is the reality of creation fully revealed in the mystery of God. Pope John Paul II reminded us of this in a visit to the alpine summit of Adamello:

> The mountains have always held a special fascination for my heart: they invite us to climb not only materially, but also spiritually toward the realities that do not fade.... Here it truly happens that thought, in contemplating creation and even penetrating into the wonderful order of the entire universe, becomes a prayer of adoration and of trustful abandonment ... on these immaculate heights, as we renew the sacrifice of the cross, we find ourselves really united with Christ the Lord, who has loved us and given himself for us.[8]

Pope John Paul experienced mystical union with Christ, and did so as a lover of the mountains. His secret? To contemplate the glory of God with a Marian heart of receptivity. If

---

[7] W. Lynch, *Christ and Apollo: The Dimensions of the Literary Imagination* (Wilmington: ISI Books, 2004), 148.

[8] L. Zani and M. Simoneschi, *The Secret Life of John Paul II*, trans. Matthew Sherry (Charlotte, N.C.: Saint Benedict Press, 2012), 105–6.

we are ever to know these heights and depths of the spiritual life, it too must begin with a *fiat*.

When I lived in Rome, I never wanted phone calls from the States in the morning. Being the middle of the night back home, it always meant something was wrong. Such was the case five years ago, when my sister called to tell me that Dad had had a massive stroke. I flew home to find him lying in an ICU, half-paralyzed and unable to speak. It was the greatest of shocks, because no one lived a more disciplined and healthy life than our father. But such was the reality of that night, when the life of our family was forever changed.

In the months that followed, my dad set to his rehabilitation with the focused intensity of a West Point plebe. He learned again to speak and walk, recovering the basic functioning of human life. But his life had changed, his limitations now permanent. Never again would he know the adventure and romance that marked his first sixty-three years.

From his living room chair, my dad watched my adventures on fourteeners and prayed for my safety on the Colorado Trail. Though he was no longer with me in body, he was there in spirit. No one will ever teach me more about what it means to be a man than the way he embraced his limitations. He embodies the school I found on the Colorado Trail; that we learn to love precisely in and through our dependence on others and in acknowledging our need for God in all things. My dad, who can now do so little, is the greatest of adventurers.

Since I stepped off the Colorado Trail and finished Mass on the fourteeners, people have asked me what is next. I don't believe in bucket lists, and as I get older, I find achievements empty and fleeting. What I do know is this:

that the purpose of life is not adventure—the purpose of adventure is love. I will go into the backcountry with full vigor of soul for as long as there is strength in my body. But when the day comes for me to step off the trail, I hope I can do so like my dad, with humble reverence and gratitude. For as Christians we know the secret to all things: that in the Incarnation of Jesus Christ, we have humanity, creation, and God. And this is only a taste of the heights and depths that await us in Heaven.

For now, we'll see where the trail takes us. And I'll hold to the everlasting wisdom of Father Gawronski: "As Christians we don't know where we are going, but we know the Way."

INDEX